Mitzllal
STRANGER AMONG SISTERS

RACHEL DARAR LEBOWITZ

Mitzllal
STRANGER
AMONG SISTERS

AN ETHIOPIAN WOMAN'S
STRUGGLE FOR SERENITY UPON
HER RETURN TO JERUSALEM

Copyright © 2015 by Israel Bookshop Publications

ISBN 978-1-60091-380-8

All rights reserved. No part of this book may be reproduced or transmitted in any form or by any means (electronic, photocopying, recording or otherwise) without prior permission of the publisher.

Published by:
Israel Bookshop Publications
501 Prospect Street
Lakewood, NJ 08701
Tel: (732) 901-3009 / Fax: (732) 901-4012
www.israelbookshoppublications.com
info@israelbookshoppublications.com

Printed in the United States of America

Distributed in Israel by:
Shanky's
Petach Tikva 16
Jerusalem
972-2-538-6936

Distributed in Europe by:
Lehmanns
Unit E Viking Industrial Park
Rolling Mill Road
Jarrow, Tyne & Wear NE32 3DP
44-191-430-0333

Distributed in Australia by:
Gold's Book and Gift Company
3-13 William Street
Balaclava 3183
613-9527-8775

Distributed in South Africa by:
Kollel Bookshop
Northfield Centre
17 Northfield Avenue
Glenhazel 2192
27-11-440-6679

This book is dedicated in memory of

the dear souls who, with tremendous effort, succeeded in fulfilling the dream of coming to Jerusalem, though they are no longer with us:

Getahon Tesfay ben Maherete *a"h*
Avrehet Mershe bat Siveta *a"h*
Zahe Belli ben Asge *a"h*

And dedicated in memory of the dear souls who died in Ethiopia without ever fulfilling their dream:

Belli Mekonen ben Averash *a"h*
Asegesh Germay bat Taish *a"h*
Kahsai Belli ben Asegesh *a"h*
Pekado Getahon ben Avrehet *a"h*

And to all Ethiopian Jewry who trudged by foot, climbed mountains, and traversed rivers, in the hottest of desert suns, driven by their thirst to fulfill their dream.

May their souls be bound up in the bond of life!

Dedication

I would like to dedicate this book to **Dr. Yaakov Faitlovitch z"l,** an expert on Ethiopian society who studied the history and culture of our people and did everything in his power to bridge the gap between the Jews of Ethiopia and the State of Israel, as well as with our fellow Jews. Dr. Faitlovitch devoted his life to the Jews of Ethiopia and brought us into the mainstream of Jewish history.

Dr. Yaakov Faitlovitch was born in 1881 in Lodz, Poland, and passed away in 1955 in Tel Aviv. He was fluent in Hebrew, several European languages, as well as some of the dialects common in Ethiopia including Gez, Amharit, Tigris, and others. In 1904 he went on a research expedition to Ethiopia, and from then until the last days of his life, he was devoted to the Jews of Ethiopia. He visited Ethiopia a number of times following his initial journey and contributed greatly to the growth and development of the "Beta Yisrael." (The "House of Israel" is the term used by Jews of Ethiopia to define their community.) His efforts culminated in Operations Moshe and Shlomo, wherein the Jews of Ethiopia were flown to Eretz Yisrael.

Thanks to the efforts of Dr. Faitlovitch, who devoted his life to the wellbeing of the Jews of Ethiopia, we merited with Hashem's help to fulfill our thousand-year-old dream to settle in Eretz Yisrael. There are not enough words to express our gratitude.

His memory should be for a blessing.

In Dedication to

Rebbetzin Aidel Mund a"h,

Whose warm heart, big smile, and kind words always brought a smile to my face.

Acknowledgments

Thank you:

To the land of my birth that showed me and all the Beta Yisrael who we are and where our place was so that we shouldn't forget our identity. My thanks to Eretz Yisrael, Land of My Forefathers, that I acquired with much suffering.

To the *rabbanim* and tzaddikim, *Hakadosh Baruch Hu's* faithful messengers, who set aside time, thought, and effort to do the right thing before Hashem and their fellow Jews. I saw you attending to whatever you needed to attend to, from the simplest to the most complex, and I am following, with confidence, in your footsteps.

To all the amazing messengers, in all of your guises, who helped me to reconnect with the faith and trust I had lost along the way.

To all those who filled in the gaps in my knowledge. I am surrounded by truly G-d-fearing Jews, and I am grateful to be living among them.

To Yehudit Atara Wachsman, my neighbor and friend, who guided me toward closing the circle of the past and opening a new one in its place. You helped me tremendously. Hashem should help you in all that you do.

To Miriam Cohen, author of the book "Between Two Mothers" and the bestselling "Behind the Walls." Thank you for all the time you set aside for me to listen to my questions and to advise me in the writing of my book.

To my sisters Elisheva, Rivka, and Esther who listened, advised, supported, and spurred me on to write this story. If it weren't for you, I don't know whether I would have been able to actually sit down and write.

To my dear parents, for the *chinuch* and beautiful upbringing you gave me and my siblings. You built a home based on purity and integrity, and on warmth and appreciation for the good in people and the world. Thank you for all the time you spent helping me to explore my identity. I know it was sometimes very difficult for you. While writing this book, I made you relive the entire journey, and there were painful experiences into which you did not want me to delve, but I would not listen. I saw your tears and the pain and sadness etched on your faces, yet you allowed me to express the pain that was inside of me.

To my father- and mother-in-law for being their loving selves and always ready to help. Thank you to my mother-in-law for helping me through my first year of marriage. Without you by my side, I would have been terribly lonely. I came to know my husband through your stories and became closer to him through them. Thank you for giving me your son whom you raised with such loving care. I hope to continue in your footsteps and to be an *eizer k'negdo* to your beloved son.

To Akiva, my husband, who is always there for me, listening, supporting, and advising me with wisdom and love. Thank you for being *you*. Now I know why Hashem chose you to be my soul mate. I have learned so much through you about how to love and admire people who are different from me.

To my sweet children, Moriah, Yitzchak Chaim, Mordechai Eliyahu, Aharon Shalom, Bracha, and Shira, for the patience and understanding you showed while I was writing this book. One day, you will be able to read it, and I hope that you'll draw insights that will accompany

Acknowledgments

you throughout your lives. Remember that Hashem is always with you, in every situation, time, and place. Search for Him and see that His shadow follows you everywhere you go. Hashem should help you to grow and reach your full potential, and may your parents and Your Father in Heaven have much *nachat* from you.

Lastly, thank You Hashem for all the good You have given me, for Your constant presence in my life, for never abandoning me, and for always being with me even through my anguish. I pray that the *pasuk*, "*And make for Me a dwelling place, and I will dwell among you*," should be fulfilled through us, and may we merit that Your *Shechinah* should dwell within each of us forever.

Rachel Darar-Lebowitz
Tevet 5775

Introduction

Countless stories have been written and told about the Jews of Ethiopia. Most of the time, the story, lecture, or piece of research focuses on the harrowing journey of the Jews of Ethiopia as they walked, under unbearable conditions, until they reached Sudan. From there, they were flown to Eretz Yisrael.

That aspect of the story is no doubt an important element in the chronicles of the Jews of Ethiopia, and there is no person without his or her own version of the journey. Many of us lost family members along the way, and many others have no idea until today what befell the loved ones they left behind. Guilt, pain, suffering, and fear dogged our steps, but in spite of all these difficulties, there was the unshakable belief that we were doing the right thing.

The story of my life is different from other stories that have been told. Even though my journey was just as long and difficult as that of anyone else, my point of view is completely different.

I would like to invite all of you to accompany Mitzllal, the four-year-old girl who crossed raging rivers and arid deserts, climbed mountains whose narrow cliffs meant that one wrong step would result in a fall into the abyss, and traversed paths no wider than a handbreadth. The way was long and hard, and to my eyes, it seemed endless. My body was exhausted, depleted of all energy, the fatigue was indescribable, and my eyes were begging to rest. My feet could barely move at times, and I had wounds that had no time to heal. But young Mitzllal kept walking. With nearly superhuman strength, she fought the despair that threatened to overtake her. Through it all, she managed to weather all the difficulties, and she reached her destination in one piece.

But the actual passage was only the first part of my journey, the *easiest* part. The real story of the young girl began when she was seven years old. Mitzllal, now called Rachel, began to search for her true identity that, unlike the first journey that took two years, continued for sixteen full years.

It began the day that I was informed that I was "*safek Yehudi*," that my identity as a Jew was not a foregone conclusion, as I had always believed, and was now being called into question. From the moment this doubt was introduced to me, I felt like there was a black cloud hovering over my head. This awoke within me a powerful need to search for my true identity. It was a painful journey, and only at its end did I experience true peace of mind and soul.

Everything that a person experiences in his or her life, all thoughts and actions, are connected in one way or another to the identity of that person and to the roots of his or her faith. The sense of belonging a person feels gives him or her a tremendous amount of strength and fortitude. If this is the power of a basic identity, how much more so is the power of a *Jewish* identity.

It was this feeling of identity that gave the Jews of Ethiopia the strength they needed to withstand the rigors of the journey and arrive after a long *galut* to the destination of their dreams: Eretz Yisrael. Men, women, and children willingly undertook the months-long journey, with many of them sacrificing their lives along the way. Thousands met their end in the sands of the desert and were buried there alone, in the middle of nowhere, and without any of the honor due to them. Their

Introduction

loved ones carried their mourning in their hearts as they kept moving forward to fulfill the dream after thousands of years of longing. This collective sacrifice was the result of our strong Jewish identity. The Jews of Ethiopia have always fiercely guarded their Jewish identity throughout much persecution and with great difficulty.

Just like a root nourishes the entire plant, so it is with identity. If the root is intact, a person's entire being is strengthened from it. The moment the root is damaged, the entire plant is endangered. When a person's identity is called into question, the damage it causes is immeasurable. He or she will attempt to latch on to anything that might help guard the last vestige of his or her true identity that lodges in the soul. That's why so many Jews of Ethiopia cling to the heart-wrenching yet heroic stories of our journey to Eretz Yisrael, and that is why I, too, set out on my long and painful journey to discover my lost identity. I was guarding my Jewish soul so that its light shouldn't be extinguished. *Baruch Hashem*, I found what I was searching for.

I am sharing the story of my life for my fellow Jews of Ethiopia, who will certainly be able to identify with my story, and also for Jews the world over. Each person has his or her own story and unique path. It is my hope that every Jew finds his way back to his true identity, to the root of his soul, to the Jewish heart that dwells within him. I was so fortunate, after sixteen years of searching, to discover my eternal identity, and I only pray that my fellow Jews never despair and never give up until they have reconnected with their Source. If I succeed in helping even one Jew discover his unique identity, I will have fulfilled my goal for writing this book—that the greatness of my Creator should be revealed.

The Jewish people are unique and special. The Hebrew word for Jew, "*Yehudi*," comes from the Hebrew word for glorious, majestic. It also comes from the word for echo, "*hed.*" When a Jew opens his mouth and calls out before the *Ribono Shel Olam* with all his heart, he merits an echo from Heaven in return: *"I have heard your voice call out to Me, and I will help you."* But when a Jew does not cry out to Hashem, the only voice he will hear is his own, and he will be left to fend for himself.

I raised my voice. I called out to Hashem: "I'm a Jew! Abba, I'm a Jew!" My voice echoed, and I was heard. I connected with my true essence. It should be Hashem's will that we should all merit His help in finding our true path.

CHAPTER ONE

Why Does It Hurt You So Much?

"Ima, can we go to Ayalon Park today?" my five-year-old son asked me. He waited for my reply with cheerful anticipation. Taking into account all I had to do and whether or not I had the energy for it, I concluded that I wouldn't be able to fulfill his request that day.

"I'm very tired," I answered. "But we can definitely go to the park behind the house." His smile faded into a look of disappointment, but he took my reply in stride. He rode his bicycle out into the park, his little brother trailing after him.

I gathered up the rest of the children and set out for the park. It was a warm and sunny day, not too hot, and the park was full of children playing on the slides and the monkey bars.

While I was watching my children play, I heard a familiar voice calling my name. "Rachel," said my friend Yehudit. "How are you?" I made room for her on the bench, and she sat down next to me.

Yehudit is very wise, and I love to listen and learn from her. I'm not the kind of person who opens up easily, and there aren't that many people with whom I feel comfortable to share aspects of my personal life, but Yehudit was different. I've always trusted her and felt that she could help me. I'm inquisitive by nature, and her answers often brought more questions in their wake. No matter how much I prodded her, though, Yehudit always had an answer for me.

We were in the middle of an ongoing discussion that had stretched out over several weeks. As hard as Yehudit tried to give me the answers I needed, I still wasn't satisfied. I had the feeling that something was missing, but I couldn't put my finger on what it was.

This time, Yehudit responded differently to me than she had in the past. This time, it was she who asked me a question, and I could think of no reply. The words she uttered were just what I needed to hear: "Why does it hurt you so much?"

Yehudit noticed how surprised I was at her inquiry; I had come to expect answers from her, not questions. "You need to explore why this troubles you so much," she told me. I remained silent, but within me, my voice started to be heard.

In the midst of my turmoil, I realized it was getting late and my baby had fallen asleep in the stroller. I gathered up the children, and we returned home. After they were all asleep, I sat down with my husband, Akiva, and we talked about our day, as was our nightly ritual. My husband shared his excitement with me over finishing *Masechet Ketubot*. "There will be a *siyum* to celebrate. Let's find a babysitter, and we'll go together," he said. I was so happy for him. We finalized our plans, but when he asked me how my day was, I told him about my conversation with Yehudit and the question she had asked me. We spoke about it until he had to leave to *daven* Ma'ariv and for night *seder*.

After finishing my housework, I sat down on the couch with my favorite magazine and waited for my husband to return home. I tried to read, but I couldn't concentrate, and I found myself reading each line two or three times. I set the magazine down, unread, on the couch next to me, leaned my head back, and closed my eyes. As was my habit, I made an accounting of my day so that I could make a better tomorrow.

Like a film strip, I began to see pictures of everything that had happened throughout the day. The images flashed by, and I observed them objectively, asking myself what went well and what could be improved. What did I accomplish and what still needed doing? Was it right for me to rebuke my son, or should I have just kept quiet? Did I listen to my husband and my children and give them everything they needed?

But out of all the images that passed by, one stood out and wouldn't let me close my eyes. Yehudit's question appeared before me once again: *"Why does it hurt you so much?"*

My nature abhors leaving matters unresolved, so I tried to give this troubling picture a name. I knew I had to find the answer to this question, and in the process, I found myself transported back in time to thirty years earlier, so far from where I was now and so close to the place I'd called home. Among the happy voices of children playing in the park, I could also hear the fearful and threatening voices calling out to me from the land of my birth.

CHAPTER TWO

A Not So Distant Past

By the time I was seven, I had already crossed over the borders of Ethiopia and come to Eretz Yisrael. One would have thought that the chapter of my life labeled "Ethiopia" had come to an end and a new chapter was beginning, but this was not the case. The aftershocks of my life in Ethiopia continued to have a crucial effect on every aspect of my life.

At a certain point, I realized that in this new place I had come to, Eretz Yisrael, my Jewish identity was being called into question. The uncertainty colored my entire life and moved me to try to understand the roots of those who lived long before me. My curiosity took me directly to the source of my roots, and most important, to the acceptance of myself exactly as I was, regardless of the status of my identity. I understood that with my honorable ancestry standing behind me, I could hold my head up with strong Jewish pride and without the fear of standing out.

Ethiopia, known in the Tanach as Kush, is an ancient land that was settled over two thousand years ago. Throughout the centuries, many different tribes dwelled there and devoted themselves to the land. There is a rich variety of nations, cultures, customs, and languages in Ethiopia, and it is this diversity that attracts researchers, tourists, and travelers to its borders.

The Jews of Ethiopia lived in wooden cabins that were situated near a source of water. They were spread out in villages, with an extended family group dominating each village. They earned their living either as farmers, blacksmiths, or weavers. These occupations were typical for Jews because the non-Jews lacked the tools necessary for them. The women took care of the children and the household and also made pottery. The boys were taught to tend sheep and cows from a very early age, and the girls helped with the housework. They were a united people who believed in Hashem and kept the mitzvot of Shabbat, Yamim Tovim, the blessing of the new moon, *brit milah*, and *taharat hamishpachah* under incredibly difficult conditions. Their devotion to keeping these mitzvot distinguished them from the non-Jews who surrounded them.

Sometime during the ninth century, a merchant named Eldad ha-Dani passed through Ethiopia on his way to North Africa. Upon his arrival, he described his encounter with the descendants of the Dan Tribe who dwelled in Ethiopia along with members of the other ten tribes who were lost to us. Thus, the Jewish world in North Africa was informed of the existence of members of the lost tribes in the land of Kush. It had never occurred to anyone that just beyond the rivers of Kush lived a glorious nation of Jews who called themselves the Beta Yisrael.

From the writings of Eldad ha-Dani:

When Yeravam ben Nevat became king and wished to cause his subjects to sin, he set up two golden calves. At that time, the House of David was divided, and the northern tribes cried, "Let us go wage war against Rechavam and Yerushalayim." Others, however, answered, "Why shall we fight our own brethren, and against the son of our master David?" Nevertheless, the elders of Israel said that since Dan had the greatest prowess in battle, they should lead the army against Yehudah. Dan, however, answered, "By the life of our forefather Dan, we will not battle our brethren in Yehudah, nor cause their blood to be spilled."

They took their axes, spears, and bows, and endangered themselves by leaving Eretz Yisrael, for they saw that it was impossible to stay. They said to themselves, "If we leave now, we shall choose our new residence; should we stay, eventually others will take us away."

Finally, they were advised to head toward Egypt, but not on the same path that our forefathers took when they left, and also not in order to destroy it, only to cross the Pishon (Nile) River into Ethiopia.

When they entered Egypt, they caused great consternation among the Egyptians. The Egyptians sent delegations inquiring if they were there for peaceful purposes or to do battle. They answered that they came in peace and only wished to cross their borders into Ethiopia, where they hoped to find rest. Nevertheless, the Egyptians would not believe them and remained at their posts until they passed through their land and reached Ethiopia. There they found a large and fertile country with fields, vineyards, gardens, and orchards.

The residents did not prevent the Danites from settling there. They lived there for many years until they owned great wealth, and they multiplied greatly. These four tribes, Dan, Naftali, Gad, and Asher, are encamped in the country of Chavilah, where gold is to be found. These are good and secure lands in the kingdom of Farium, which is in the empire of Horinus. They rely on Hashem, and He has helped them. When they wish, they travel to the other edge of their land, an area of two days' travel in each direction. They never camp on the paths, only in fields or vineyards. They are of perfect faith, and their Talmud is in Hebrew. When they study, they preface their statements with the words, "So our rabbis taught us, who received this from Yehoshua bin Nun, whose wisdom came from the mouth of our father Moshe, from the mouth of Hashem." They don't know the names of the rabbis, for they lived during the time of the second Beit Hamikdash and, therefore, were unknown to them. They *speak only Hebrew, constantly purify themselves, and never swear oaths. If anyone mentions Hashem's Name in vain, they will admonish him that this sin causes one's children to die young.*

The validity of Eldad ha-Dani's controversial account was still being debated by the *Geonim* in the tenth century, but most of the *chachamim* of the time, including Rav Tzemach Gaon, Rav Yaakov Castro, Rashi in *Sefer Pardes*, the Rabad in *Sefer Eshkol*, the Rambam, the *Ba'alei Tosafos* and others, validated the account.

Either way, the story of the Jewish merchant Eldad ha-Dani spread throughout North Africa, providing the foundation for the first halachic ruling regarding the origin and identity of those who dwelled in Kush. The Ridbaz stated: "There are three kingdoms in Kush. Some of them are Yishmaelites, some are Aramaic, and some are Jews from Shevet Dan. Those who come from Kush are without a doubt from Shevet Dan, and because there were no *chachamim* and *Ba'alei Kabbalah* among them, they interpreted the Torah in a literal way."

The period of time Eldad ha-Dani was referring to was the golden age of the Beta Yisrael. Although this vibrant kingdom was continually being oppressed by their Christian neighbors, causing the era to be referred to as the "Dark Age of Ethiopia," its glory could not be dimmed.

Eventually enormous changes took place. The kingdom collapsed, wars broke out, and the Jewish population decreased drastically. The Jews of Ethiopia remained cut off from their fellow Jews in Eretz Yisrael for hundreds of years. The contributions of *chachamim* during that period enhanced and enriched the Torah world. The *rabbanim* were afraid that with the passing of time, the Oral Torah would be forgotten, so they committed to writing down its meanings and explanations as a guideline for future generations. The First and Second Temples were destroyed, and the Jews were dispersed throughout the world, but they kept both the Written and the Oral Torah, thanks to the foresight of the *rabbanim*. All the Jews remained unified despite their dispersal, and it was only the Jews of Ethiopia who were cut off.

While the Beta Yisrael were once highly esteemed in Ethiopia, they soon became persecuted. Their pursuers did everything in their power to harm them. They attacked them physically, plundered their possessions, and robbed them of their identity and individuality, their sole intent being to eradicate them. The population of the Beta Yisrael began to dwindle, either by death or by those who sought a new identity in order to save themselves, but others clung to their identity despite great odds. The underlying motive behind all the persecution boiled down to one thing: religion.

By the end of the eighteenth century, the news of the existence of the Beta Yisrael had spread throughout the entire world. The news traveled by word of mouth as researchers, tourists, missionaries, and other travelers streamed into the African continent from every corner of the world. Up until this time, the Jews of Ethiopia were convinced they were the last Jews on earth.

In 1848 a letter was sent from the Beta Yisrael to the Jews of Europe, reminding them that they were waiting for the coming of Mashiach in order to be united with the rest of the Jewish nation. A year later, they sent Daniel ben Chananya and his son Moshe from Ethiopia to Eretz Yisrael. This was the beginning of an exchange of letters between the Jews of the world and the Beta Yisrael.

These letters contained heartfelt pleas from the Beta Yisrael to save them from the claws of Christian missionaries. The first one to act on their behalf was Dr. Azriel Hildesheimer. He wrote several letters to important rabbis on behalf of the Beta Yisrael, convincing them to issue a call to action that was published in Jewish newspapers throughout

Europe. This call resulted in the selection of Yosef HaLevi to travel to Ethiopia to visit and provide aid to the Beta Yisrael.

Yosef HaLevi arrived in Ethiopia in 5627 (1867) and met with the local Jewish community. Upon his return to Europe, he publicized information about the community he'd gotten to know.

For the forty years following Yosef HaLevi's visit, there were no further delegations to Ethiopia, which resulted in a greater isolation between the two exiles. In the year 5664 (1904), Dr. Yaakov Faitlovitch, a student of HaLevi, was sent to Ethiopia with the blessing of the Chief Rabbi of Tzfat, Harav Tzadok Cohen. Dr. Faitlovitch became the main conduit connecting the Beta Yisrael and the Jews of Europe until his death in 5715 (1955). Dr. Faitlovitch reawakened the dormant connection between the communities, and the correspondence between them was reinstated. During the years 5696 (1936) and 5701 (1941), communication was temporarily halted due to the conquest of Ethiopia by Italy.

The subject of the lost tribes in Ethiopia drew the attention of Dr. Faitlovitch, and the redemption of these Jews became the focus of his life's work. Among his many contributions was the establishment of a school for the Beta Yisrael in Addis Ababa. When he returned to Europe, he brought along two youths from the Beta Yisrael, Gatya Yermiyahu and Tamarat Emanuel, in order to provide them with a traditional Jewish education that they would then be able to pass on to their fellow Ethiopians. In fact, Tamarat Emanuel returned to Ethiopia in 5683 (1923) and organized a training school for teachers, and as a close associate of Haile Selassie, found many ways to benefit the Jews.

Throughout his travels, Dr. Faitlovitch continued to concentrate his efforts on behalf of the Jews of Ethiopia wherever he went. He met with important Jewish leaders and with anyone with any connection to the Jews of Ethiopia, including diplomats stationed in Ethiopia, Egypt, and Europe. He even received support for his missions from Baron Rothschild and the Kol Yisrael Chaverim organization, as well as letters of recommendation and support for his research from *rabbanim* in Eretz Yisrael.

Dr. Faitlovitch's efforts were focused on education and the establishment of schools for the Beta Yisrael. He also studied their customs and traditions and successfully influenced them to observe more mitzvot, in addition to introducing them to the Talmud. Under his influence, the people of the Beta Yisrael changed their religious customs.

His efforts gave them hope that they would overcome their battle with the missionaries who sought their conversion to Christianity. To this end, he wrote five letters—*Igrat Falashim, Igrat Shalom, Igrat M'vaser, Igrat Tanchumim,* and *Igrat Achvah*—and distributed them throughout the villages. The letters called upon the Beta Yisrael to remain strong in their commitment to Judaism and resist conversion.

There is much to be learned from Dr. Faitlovitch's reports documenting the customs of the Beta Yisrael at the beginning of the twentieth century. He testified to the existence of communities that were decimated forty years earlier during the reign of Kapu Kahn ("The Reign of Terror"), and it is only the names of the villages and tales from the neighboring communities that keep their memory alive.

In 5733 (1973), a devastating famine struck Ethiopia, and at the same time, allegations of corruption and immorality were brought against the upper echelons of the government. Millions of farmers were left starving for bread. A revolt rose up against the government, aided and abetted by students, farmers, soldiers, and others.

Mengistu Haile Mariam, the head of the army, garnered wide support from these protestors. In the end, the uprising succeeded to oust

Selassie, imprison him, and execute members of the government. In 5735 (1975), Selassie died under mysterious circumstances, and from 5737 (1977) on, war broke out frequently in Ethiopia. Mengistu Haile Mariam, now the leader of the country, was violent and unscrupulous and did not hesitate to execute whoever stood in his path. His rule brought a cruel end to those who opposed him. This period was later known as "The Red Terror."

The Beta Yisrael had endured thousands of years of isolation, distance, and disconnection from their Jewish brethren, yet they guarded their Judaism in spite of these daunting obstacles. When they were finally introduced to the rest of their brethren around the world, the verse (*Bamidbar* 23:9), "*It is a nation that will dwell in solitude and not be reckoned among the nations,*" was fulfilled. In spite of the difficulty that came along with abandoning their homeland, they were willing to do anything to guard their Judaism.

The Jews of Ethiopia had dreamed of coming to Eretz Yisrael for thousands of years. Like the sun that rises each morning and lights up the entire world, the dream accompanied them constantly and illuminated their days.

Like the sun that never changes its nature, always rising in the east and setting in the west, the dream never faltered and its hue never faded. Now, finally, their dream was going to be fulfilled, and in their hearts, they still found it hard to believe. Was the dream really going to come true?

CHAPTER THREE

My Parents' Home

My father was born in the village of Adi Teleke in the Tigrei region, home to nine families who identified themselves as members of the Beta Yisrael. My parents built their house there after they were married. The houses were built close together, between thirty and a hundred feet apart from each other and about three to six hundred feet from our Christian and Muslim neighbors.

There are more than seventy different languages spoken in Ethiopia. The official language is Amharit, but we spoke Tigris in our village. The Jews and non-Jews lived separately, each according to their beliefs, peacefully and without persecution. The non-Jews would invite their Jewish neighbors to their celebrations, and sensitive to the fact that the Jews could not eat their food, supplied them with a cow prior to the celebration so it could be prepared according to their customs. Although relations between the two groups were cordial, their differences were glaringly obvious. The Jews stuck together, united in the belief that their true homeland was far from Ethiopia.

Our house was built from chiseled stones, in contrast to the other houses that were made from straw. The roof was made from metal, and its edges extended beyond the walls of the house to protect it from the rain. Besides the house we lived in, we had a second smaller house used to store grain and host guests.

The house we lived in had one large room and a door made of

My Parents' Home

wood. There were two windows for smoke ventilation. Large ceramic storage vessels separated the kitchen from the living room, and two beds that looked like long, wide concrete shelves were attached to the wall. Between the beds was a *sanduk*, a large crate that held clothing and jewelry. Our kitchen items—the *finjel*, small coffee cups the size of espresso cups, and the *jebena*, a special coffee pot made out of black clay—were kept on a row of shelves along the wall. Underneath these shelves were colorful straw rings my mother made that were used as placemats for the coffee cups. Straw baskets of different sizes were stored on other shelves, as well as pots made from gourd, the *metniya* (milking pot), the *megogo* (frying pan), the *mukecha* (a small mortar made from the trunk of a tree), and spices such as *chorecho* (salt), and *berbereh* (hot pepper).

A coal-burning oven made from clay filled the center of the main room. We used it to cook, boil water, and warm the house in the winter. On hot summer days, we always cooked outside to avoid overheating the house.

Against the wall were benches called *medev*. Near them stood the most beautiful and precious item in the house: the *mesov*. This was a straw table that stood about three feet high, a multi-colored work of art with yellow, green, red, orange, blue, and white straw woven together in an intricate design. This prized wedding gift stood on a cone-shaped base and expanded into a round table. The table had a cover with a handle in the middle to preserve the food.

Saba Getahun and Savta Avrehet, my father's parents, lived directly across from our house. Children were not allowed to use their grandparents' real names, so we called Savta Avrehet by the name Savta Adiyeh. My uncle Chagos lived about fifty feet away. The three houses shared a large, fenced-in courtyard we occasionally used for Shabbat gatherings, holidays, and celebrations, as well as to house our sheep when they weren't grazing. We also built a *das*, a large sukkah-like structure made from branches. Family celebrations occasionally drew our Christian and Muslim neighbors, and they would sit in the sukkah, eating and drinking and taking part in our celebrations. For most of the holidays, Jews from all over streamed toward the village where the *kes* (religious leader) lived. They recited special prayers accompanied by a lilting melody. The *kes* taught halachah and offered words of inspiration and encouragement, reassuring them that the longed-for day would soon come when they would go up to Yerushalayim. These talks injected the people with renewed strength to hold on in spite of all obstacles, danger, and tribulations they continually faced.

After the *kahal* returned home to their villages, they tried to remain on the path of the *kes*, encouraging each other and giving *shiurim* from the *sefer Metzchaf*. Every Shabbat, they would arrange *mechber*, gatherings, each family in turn. When it was my father's turn for *mechber*, he would build a big sukkah in the courtyard, and everyone would gather there.

There were two entrances to our courtyard. The one on the right led out to the cornfield. At one time, it was filled with rocks, stones, thorns, and weeds, but with the help of others, my father cleaned it up and planted corn seeds. The cornfield was so beautiful that its formerly barren state was soon forgotten. Soft green grass grew on a piece of land past the cornfield, and our sheep grazed there. Beyond the grassland, the Katin Klay River ran through a section of brown earth sealed off from the lush greenery and between two hills dotted with houses belonging to the villagers. The river was about six feet wide, but it was so shallow that even small children were able to cross it, except where it flowed downward and gathered into a small, deep pool.

CHAPTER FOUR

Welcome News

In 5733 (1973), a halachic decision in Jerusalem was announced, ruling that the Beta Yisrael were descendants of the Tribes of Israel that had migrated southward to Kush and needed to be rescued immediately before assimilation and aggressive missionary activity took their toll on the population. It was urgent they be brought to Eretz Yisrael where they could receive a Torah education and participate in the building of Eretz Yisrael. The only caveat, included in the original decision, was that the Jews of Ethiopia were to be considered *safek Yehudi*, of questionable Jewish identity, and they would be obligated to undergo *giyur l'chumrah*, a conversion ceremony employed in situations where the facts are not perfectly clear. A controversy broke out in the wake of the ruling, and the vexing question of "Who is a Jew?" raised its head once again.

In 5735 (1975), two years after this decision was announced, the Law of Return was invoked regarding the Jews of Ethiopia, and the Beta Yisrael were set to begin a new chapter in their lives. Their longing for Jerusalem strengthened and grew.

The devastating famine that ravaged Ethiopia began in 5733 (1973) and reached its highest point during 5744–5745 (1984–1985). The death toll in Sudan rose at an alarming rate as people died of hunger, disease, and plague. The Beta Yisrael were disparaged as opportunists in the media, which claimed that the Jews only wanted to go to Israel as a way to escape their suffering. This erroneous allegation conveniently ignored the fact that the Jews had already begun their pilgrimage from Ethiopia eight years before the famine began.

At the same time, war broke out between the Democrats and the Communists. Fear and terror spread through the streets, and the urgency for the Beta Yisrael to leave Ethiopia reached critical levels.

Along with the anticipation of all the Beta Yisrael to fulfill their centuries-long dream, my family was also in suspense. It was 5736 (1976), and my mother was expecting a baby. My parents left Adi Teleke and traveled to my grandmother's house in Adi Abu, where she could attend to my mother before and after the birth.

Within a short time, a pure and innocent cry rang out suddenly throughout the house, a glaring contrast to the sounds of war taking place just outside. The precious noise helped my family briefly forget their worries as the joy of a new baby joining the family and the Beta Yisrael was immeasurable.

Ima carefully scrutinized my face as she held me in her arms, trying to decide who I looked like. My skin was light brown, my face was long and narrow, my hair was sparse and black, and my fingers were long and slim. My mother examined them and noticed that my hands were not clenched into fists as it is with most babies; they were open and unfurled. A smile broke out on my mother's face as she declared, "This baby will be giving and generous! Look at her hands! They are wide open, a sign that her heart will also be open and that she'll listen to all who are needy." She wrapped me in the *shash*, a long piece of white cotton, and held me close to her.

Afterward, Ima looked at me, my big black eyes dominating my face, and decided that I looked like both my mother and my father!

Women came to wish mazel tov and suggest names for the baby. A name is very significant and is neither given lightly nor without

Welcome News

thought. None of the names mentioned appealed to my mother, until my great-aunt Amoi Bayish (Saba Gatahun's sister) suggested the name Mitzllal. My mother immediately liked the suggestion. The name Mitzllal is from the word "*tzlal*," whose root means "shadow," and my aunt added her blessing: "May Hashem spread His sheltering shadow over this child, and may Hashem spread His shadow over her parents, and may joy and happiness be your lot." This meaningful name made my mother very happy. She recalled the stories her mother had told her when she was a child, detailing the suffering her ancestors had undergone to guard this *tzlal*. At the time of my birth, the Beta Yisrael were in danger, and Ima prayed that we should continue to shelter under Hashem's wings as we had until now. My parents were deeply affected by my name and all it implied, alluding to a past laden with trials and tribulations and battles waged with characteristic Jewish tenacity to guard the right to practice our religion. The name also alluded to the present, that even at this precise moment of *tzlal*, the sounds of war and the pounding of running feet could be heard at the same time. My parents didn't allow external circumstances to dictate the course of their lives, and as far as they were concerned, as miraculous as it was, they were still sheltered in the shadow of Hashem's wings.

At the end of several weeks' stay, my parents returned home. My brother Nogosa, then two years old, rode on a donkey. Ima wrapped me in her arms, and my parents entered the house with a new baby in their hands. Life as they knew it would be changed forever.

CHAPTER FIVE

A Day in the Life of an Ethiopian Family

I have a few vivid memories of my life in Ethiopia. Whatever was missing from my own memories was provided by the many stories Ima told me throughout my childhood.

In the courtyard of our home were chickens that would wake Ima every morning with the sounds of their crowing. With her usual alacrity, she would start to grind the *teff*, which is a vitamin-filled type of grain unique to Ethiopia. To grind it, she used a large mortar and pestle that stood beside the house, and after adding water prepared the night before, left it to ferment in a large container. Meanwhile, she would take some branches that were piled up close to the house, lay them on the clay oven, and light them. Ima then put the *megogo* (large frying pan) on top of the fire. The wood burned, the frying pan warmed up, and with a bowl and ladle, she'd spoon the brown mixture into circles on the frying pan. She knew it was ready when it would begin to bubble on top, and she would then put it aside in a large bowl. This was how the flat, round *injera* were made. *Injera* comprised the main component of our diets. It was eaten every day with different combinations: with stewed lentils, with chicken, with meat, with vegetables, or with dairy.

By this time, Abba would already be dressed, and he would greet Ima with a question: "*Dachan du chadirki*? (Did you sleep well?)" Ima would reply, "*Yizgaviher Yemezgen*. (Hashem should be blessed.)" She would then ask how he was, and he would reply the same way. After this exchange, she would put a large bowl of water before him. Abba would rinse his hands, dry them with a towel, and then he would begin his morning prayers.

After this Ima would prepare the *chebchi*, a meat stew. She'd fry onions in a wide pot and add spices, mainly hot pepper. She would then add small cubes of meat, mix it well, and leave it to simmer on the fire. Meanwhile, she'd go inside the house, take a bag of clothes and a pitcher, and go down to the river. There, she'd remove the clothes from the bag and wash them well before wringing them out and putting them back in the bag. She'd then fill the pitcher with water and turn toward home. Sometimes she would meet other women by the river, occasionally on the way home, and sometimes she wouldn't see anyone at all. When she'd near the house, she'd take the clothes from the bag and spread them out to dry on the tree nearest to the house or on the rocks and stones if there wasn't enough room. After she'd finish, she'd go back inside.

By this time I'd be awake. Ima would pick me up and carry me on her back, trying to finish whatever was left to do before Abba would return. Ima would turn to the bowl of fresh coffee beans, take a half a cup from the bowl, rinse them, and put them in a frying pan to roast until they turned a light brown. Abba would finish praying and would then come and take his place on the right side of the *medev*. Ima would approach Abba with the pan in her hand and would shake it from side to side to spread the delicious aroma of the coffee beans around the room. Abba enjoyed the smell of the beans and would bless Ima in her work, to which she would reply, "Amen." Then Ima would crush the coffee beans in the *mukecha* and grind them well, fill up the *jebena* (coffee pot) with water, and put the water on the fire. She would pour the coffee she had ground into a powder, then she would serve the coffee in the *finjel*, special coffee cups. She would also serve the *kolo*, a mixture of popcorn and roasted chick peas. Along with the coffee, Ima would serve *kicha*, Ethiopian bread, and she would of course set out the *itan*, incense, that spread a pleasant aroma around the house. Ima would drink three cups of coffee, and after she'd finish, she'd give Nogosa milk and *kicha* and then nurse me.

After we were fed, I'd go to sleep and Nogosa would go outside. Ima would then rinse out the coffee cups, and when Abba would finish tending to the sheep, he'd come home, Nogosa following on his heels. He would wash his hands again and sit down in his place with Nogosa at his side. Ima would pour the spicy meat stew on top of *injera* and set more *injera* on the side to scoop up the sauce. Abba would recite the blessing over the meal, and my mother and Nogosa would listen and say "Amen." Ima would start eating after Abba, and then Nogosa would eat while I slept in a *shash* on my mother's back. We didn't have a baby carriage, and sleeping on my mother's back was the easiest solution at hand. When they finished eating, they would wash their hands again and say the blessing after the meal, and then they would get up to do their various tasks. Abba would go out to work in the wheat field, Ima would be busy with her housework, and Nogosa would run out to play with the roosters.

During the winter, Abba was occupied with farming. He'd prepare the land and then plant wheat, corn, chick peas, sesame, and more. The planting was spread out over the course of half a year, and the harvest was so large that it was sometimes enough to last for two years. In the spring, Abba was busy with commerce. He would buy cattle inexpensively from distant places and sell them for a profit in our district.

CHAPTER SIX

A Time to Act

Although their lives continued to function normally, deep down, my parents knew that the time had come to take action. Many of their relatives had already abandoned their villages. They made their escapes in the middle of the night, leaving their houses empty. The mass exodus put pressure on those left behind. My parents knew they would also need to leave sooner or later and started to prepare for their departure. Abba planted only enough to produce a yield for one year, but then the year passed and they still hadn't left. The next year, they again made preparations to depart as they had the previous year, but by this time, the game had changed. Diplomatic relations between Ethiopia and Israel had broken down. Nineteen schools that had been established in the village communities in Ethiopia were shut down, Israeli researchers were expelled from Ethiopia, and the covert *aliyah* movement was halted indefinitely.

Daily life continued normally while my parents waited for the right moment to act. Meanwhile, their disappointment was tempered by the joy of another baby joining the family, my sister Alofo. Another year passed. My brother Nogosa, then four, started to tend the sheep every morning. I was two and already running around the house after my mother, my grandmother, or my brother. As I grew, I became more aware of my surroundings.

As mentioned earlier, the Jewish families gathered together on Shabbat in *mechber*. I was three years old when I attended one of these meetings for the first time. While I was playing near my house, I saw a group of people go into the sukkah in the middle of our courtyard. I didn't understand why all these people were streaming into our sukkah, and I ran home to investigate. I didn't understand the purpose of the gathering, but I clearly remember standing beside the entrance to the sukkah and seeing my father standing while everyone else was seated. Abba held a booklet in his hand, and he was reading from it and then explaining what he read to all those gathered. The men and women were whispering among themselves, and their faces were sad. The sound of sighing echoed around the room. From all the words I heard, one stood out among all the others: "Yerushalayim… Yerushalayim… Yerushalayim." I saw my mother, her head turned down and away, and her face mirroring the others' faces. I don't know how much of what I heard there I actually remembered, but that one word I kept hearing, *Yerushalayim*, entered the very core of my being together with the heartrending expressions I could see on the people's faces. They were all engraved in my heart, touching me deeply, and I guarded them as secrets of my heart.

My mother told me that when I was small, I often spent time with adults, asking them all kinds of questions, and sometimes, I chimed in with my own opinions. When that happened, Ima informed me that it wasn't nice to mix into adult conversations and ordered me to go play with children my own age. Most of the time, I remembered my mother's rebuke and kept quiet, but there were other times when I forgot myself and joined in.

When I was about three and a half, one of the neighbors came to my mother, barely able to contain her excitement. "Parda Aklum went to Sudan!" she exclaimed. "He put a letter and a picture of himself into an envelope and gave it to a man he met on the way who was happy to deliver the letter in exchange for a large fee. Along with the envelope, Parda gave him a detailed description of Adai Vurbeh, his village, and his house. This man traveled from Sudan to Adai Vurbeh and gave the envelope to Parda's family. After a few days, the family picked themselves up and left. They arrived in Sudan a few days later, and now..." the neighbor said breathlessly, "they are already in Yerushalayim!"

"So fast?" my mother asked.

"Yes! That fast!" the neighbor said, and then she and my mother went their separate ways.

In the winter of 5740 (1980), my sister Migbei was born, and Ima went to the After-Birth House. This was a special house where the women of the Beta Yisrael stayed with their babies after birth, forty days for a boy and eighty days for a girl. About two hours after the birth, my father arrived at the House with my sister Alofo and myself in tow. He placed a dish of *injera* and *tzevchi* next to a circle of stones that surrounded the After-Birth House, directly across from the entrance. It was forbidden to enter the house, because anyone who did was considered *tamei*, impure. Ima came out and took the plate inside, and when she returned, Abba told her that he was going to a *levayah*, as it was very important for him to attend.

Abba went on his way, and Alofo and I remained behind, near the circle of stones. We chatted a bit with Ima, saw the new baby, and even though we so much wanted to be with Ima and hold the baby, we knew that we were not allowed to go inside. Ima told us that we had to behave nicely until Abba returned, or we could go play at either Savta's or Uncle Chagos' house. We complied dutifully and went off to play.

The Beit Haniddah where Ima was staying was situated on a hill, and from there, Ima could not only see our house, but she could also see Nogosa tending the sheep in the grassland.

After wandering around a bit, we went to look for Nogosa and play with Merrit, our favorite cow. We passed our house, walked through the cornfield, and went down a winding path that opened out into the grassland. We looked for Nogosa and the cows, but we couldn't find them. Meanwhile, Ima was watching us from her vantage point on the hill, worried that we might go too close to the river. We saw a boy tending the sheep off in the distance, but there was still no sign of Nogosa. Suddenly, without any warning, the sky split open and rain poured down on us. We turned back and started to run with all our might back to our house, holding tightly to each other's hands. The boy we'd seen with the sheep ran past us to his house without offering to help. We followed quickly after him until we came to the winding path that led up to our house, and then we stopped dead in our tracks. The river had overflowed and made a small pool, blocking us from climbing the path to our house. When we saw the water, we began to cry, calling out for Abba and Ima to come and rescue us. Neither one of them could help us; Abba was at the *levayah*, and Ima was in the Beit Haniddah, literally watching us cry out for her! She could see that we were stuck, and her eyes filled with tears. She knew she was exactly where Hashem wanted her to be, and that Abba was also doing *ratzon Hashem* by attending the *levayah*, and there we were, two little girls desperate for someone to come and help us.

Ima told me later that the only thing she could do was close her eyes and pray for help from the One Whose will she was doing, saying, "Hashem, I am doing Your will with love and awe. I do all that You command of me with the utmost care, and I have no doubt that my place right now is here. Please, Hashem, make my will Your will, as I make Your will mine. Help my daughters! They need Your help!"

When my mother opened her eyes, she saw that her prayer had

been accepted immediately. Almost without thinking, I had hoisted my two-year-old sister onto my back and waded into the water, my sister and I holding on to each other for dear life, or more accurately, Hashem holding on to both of us and bringing us onto dry land. We were crying from fright but happy that we had made it to the other side. I put my sister down, and together, we ran toward the house while my mother watched us from the hill, grateful to Hashem that we were safe.

Ima continued to watch us even after we went inside the house. Nogosa was home, but we had no idea where he'd been or how he got there. After a while, my father returned, saw the two of us soaking wet, and asked, "Why didn't you come back home as soon as it started to rain? Why did you wait until everything was already flooded?" We didn't know how to answer him and were bewildered by his reprimand, but we were still really happy to see him.

Abba changed our clothing and my brother lit a fire. The three of us, myself, Alofo, and Nogosa, gathered together and warmed ourselves. Abba changed his clothes, boiled some water in the *jebena* and made *shahi*, tea, for all of us. We held our cups tightly in our hands and drank deeply.

Night fell, the rain slackened, and though we missed Ima terribly, our house was a beacon of light and warmth for us, our very own fortress that stood against the darkness.

CHAPTER SEVEN

Savta Indaya

My mother's mother, Savta Indaya, whose real name was Asegash, lived in the village of Adi Abu, quite far from our home. There she kept stores of honey, sheep, and cattle, and she was considered wealthy. Saba Blai Mekonen had passed away when my mother was still a child, and she had no memory of him. Savta raised six children on her own. She was a strong woman with a seemingly endless supply of energy. She was devoted to her children and raised them with wisdom and care, while simultaneously keeping house and providing for the family. She found ingenious ways to earn money, and people respected her for that. Savta was also known for her acts of kindness, particularly feeding the many hungry people who turned to her for help. Savta fed them and took care of them along with her own children.

One of our autumn visits, before my sister Migbei was born, stands out clearly in my mind. I remember Savta Indaya as being tall and thin, and it seemed to me that she had difficulty walking. There was something wrong with her foot. I remember that there were two beds in a small room, and one of the beds was about a meter (three feet) high while the other one was only about thirty centimeters (one foot) from the floor. Savta climbed down from the larger bed, and while trying to reach the smaller one, her foot lost its step, and she nearly fell. When she reached the smaller bed, she sat down and pulled me onto her lap.

During that visit, my parents spent a lot of time talking with Savta and the rest of the extended family while we cousins played together happily. Everyone enjoyed themselves by Savta Indaya's, and we would return home exhausted, but content.

Savta Indaya was deeply attached to her family and bore no small amount of heartache over them. When my mother's brother Tzahayeh made *aliyah* in 5726 (1966), he stayed in Eretz Yisrael for four years and then returned to Ethiopia. A few months later, he married and returned to Eretz Yisrael with his wife. Another brother, Geneto, made *aliyah* about a year after Tzahayeh, while his wife and two children remained in Ethiopia with Savta. When the time came for them to join their father in Eretz Yisrael, Savta accompanied them as far as she could go. While she adored all her children and grandchildren, she had a special place in her heart for Geneto's sons, Binyamin and Yissachar, and had grown very attached to them. Savta cried the entire way until they reached the point where they had to part. Savta blessed her daughter-in-law and her precious grandsons: "Good luck, and may you arrive home safely." Then, she added, "And G-d willing, we will see each other again very soon."

The moment of parting was unbearably poignant, a cascade of tears, hugs, kisses, and endless blessings. Savta began to miss them from the moment they parted. She returned home heartbroken, lay down, and drenched her pillow with her tears.

At the same time, her daughter-in-law and grandchildren were already in Addis Ababa, the first stop of their journey. Yissachar, the second grandson, lay down on his bed in one room while Binyamin slept in the other room with their mother. Yissachar suddenly realized that he was not going to see Savta again for a very long time. A twinge of longing squeezed his heart. Suddenly, a fly flew in through the window and flew around the room until it settled on the ceiling. Yissachar took note of the fly, and, awash in sadness, called out to it, "Hey, fly! Go bring my Savta Indaya here. Tell her that Yissachar loves her and misses her terribly!" He raised his eyes to the fly with hope and anticipation.

The fly spread its wings, flew around the room a bit, then flew out the window. *Maybe he's going to get Savta,* thought Yissachar. *If only!*

The next morning, as Savta awakened to the crow of the roosters, she knew she had to face the new day in spite of the difficulty of parting with family. She had to continue to live her normal life even though her son's family was making their way to a new life. She had no doubt they were doing the right thing, but that certainly didn't stop her from worrying about them and praying that they reach their destination safely.

Her pillow was still soaked with tears, but Savta knew it was time to square her shoulders and move forward. The moment she made this resolution, a very strange thing happened: Savta's foot refused to hold her up. She held on to the bed tightly and tried to stand up, but her foot chose that moment to rebel. Her children ran into her room at the sound of her screams, and to their alarm, witnessed Savta falling to the floor. From that day onward, according to my mother, Savta was paralyzed from the waist down. She would never walk again. At that point, the realization that she would never see the faces of these beloved grandchildren again overwhelmed her and brought her great pain.

CHAPTER EIGHT

A Difficult Dilemma

Winter was nearly over, and while all of our eyes were on the coming spring, the eyes of the Democratic soldiers in our village were on us. It was already afternoon on that fateful day when they informed us of a meeting being held that we were obligated to attend. The nine Jewish families who resided in the village appeared at the meeting and were greeted there by the commanding officer.

"Attention!" he said. "We have noticed that in the past few months, you have been selling off your possessions and only partly planting your fields. Where are you going? To Israel? There's no need to worry! Victory is at hand against the government, and once we triumph, your lands will be returned to you! Life will be good again! Why are you running away to Israel? There are no black Israelis! If you go, mark my words, you will become porters and street cleaners. They won't accept you there. What's so bad about living here? Stay with us! You have lived here all your lives. You are Ethiopians to your core, and now you want to abandon your homeland?"

The Democratic soldiers were trying to convince us that it would be good for us here and that we had nothing to fear.

That day, Abba came home early. We all ate supper and went to sleep, but my parents did not sleep the entire night. They and all the Beta Yisrael had waited years for this day. All the Jewish residents of Adi Teleke were united in their opinion that the day had finally come.

My uncle Mitzamihret came to my parents' house along with a few other men to confirm that my parents were also planning to leave. They had been trying to convince my parents to leave for months, and my mother finally agreed. But that very morning, my mother learned from one of her aunts that her brother Kakhsai had been imprisoned for three months already after his plan to travel to Eretz Yisrael was exposed. Uncle Kakhsai was a community activist who was accepted by Jews, Muslims, and Christians alike, and he was beloved by everyone. He had voluntarily devoted himself to serving his community for three and a half years. That evening, my mother changed her mind and declared that she would not be leaving Ethiopia. Uncle Mitzamihret and the others begged and pleaded with my parents for an entire hour, explaining, encouraging, and exhorting my parents to join them, saying, "The time has finally come!"

They finally left, but not before expressing the hope that they would meet them in two hours' time, along with the other eight families in the village who agreed to the clandestine journey.

"How can we just get up and leave at a moment's notice?" my mother asked. Abba knew exactly to what she was referring. "How can I leave my mother in the condition she is in? She lives so far away that I won't even be able to tell her good bye. Should I leave my brother in the hands of those savages and turn my head away, only to save myself? How can it be that out of all the days in the world, only now is the right time to leave?" Ima began to cry.

As she struggled to find the answers to these impossible questions, my mother remembered a song her mother used to sing to her. She repeated it to herself now as she tried to soothe her aching heart.

"*Buzot chalifna,*
Buzot sheminu,

A Difficult Dilemma

Buzot ri'ina,
R'khikna kavadina.
Anta Amlach Guytai, Na'acha amineh. Navza lemlem adi,
Beshelem a'atuvayna.
Dejifka khakipka, Mis akhatna khavusena."
(*We have been through so much,*
We have heard so much,
We have seen so much,
Far from our homeland.
You are the King, our G-d,
In You, I believe.
To the Promised Land,
Welcome us in peace.
Embrace us,
Return us to our brethren.)

Despite all the difficulties involved, Ima knew that she really didn't have a choice. Everything had already been prepared and was ready for this day. My parents had been preparing themselves to take this step. Abba had sold all his possessions, folding all the money he received into thin strips. Ima had then inserted these strips into our clothing—in the sleeves, in our collars, and alongside the buttons. Abba now exchanged our cow for a large donkey the size of a horse, and he also purchased another donkey and some horses. Everything was packed: blankets, clothing, water, matches, preserved food, popcorn kernels and chick peas, a bowl, and most important of all—flour. They included some candy for the children in one of the bags, as well. My parents prepared themselves for the expected and the unexpected at the same time, but they knew with absolute certainty that they were doing the right thing by taking the step that their ancestors were prevented from taking for different reasons. Ima understood that she had no other choice, so she gathered up her tears and took her place by my father. They both agreed that despite everything, it was now or never.

Abba and Ima were about to fulfill an ancient dream, one they had been dreaming of since they were children. Their dreams would finally be fulfilled. They would finally be joining their brothers from whom they had been separated for thousands of years! Their hearts were filled with anticipation mixed with uncertainty, but their hope and their *emunah* triumphed over all and gave them the strength to continue.

CHAPTER NINE

Where Am I Going?

Later that night, Ima awoke the three of us—Nogosa, Alofo, and myself. Migbei, my five-month-old sister, was tied on to my mother's back, secure in the *machzel* (cloth baby carrier). "Quickly, Mitzllal," my mother urged me. "Wake up!" She quickly moved on to Nogosa, who was very difficult to wake. I didn't understand what all the commotion was about, and there were so many questions I wanted to ask: Where are we going? Why are we leaving in the middle of the night? Why are we in such a hurry? I had just woken up and couldn't make any sense of what I was seeing. But as soon as I heard my mother say, "Hurry, we're going home," I remembered the Shabbat *mechber* I had attended that was engraved in my heart, where I had heard that word for the first time spoken with such awe and reverence: *Yerushalayim*. I knew one day I would know what it was, and now the moment had finally arrived.

I got up quickly. I knew that Yerushalayim was the Land of Our Fathers, a city made of gold and silver, and the people who lived there were our brothers! I heard that they were white, but couldn't figure out how that could be. I had no inkling that there were people in the world with white skin.

My mother handed me the rubber sandals she had prepared especially for the trip, and my amazement only heightened. All of these strange things were happening, and in the middle of the night! My child's mind was in a spin. Only farmers wore shoes. I had never worn shoes before in my life, having always gone barefoot. I was used to feeling the earth beneath my feet, whether it was warm or cold, whether it was dry sand, dust, or grass. They were impervious to the thorns, rocks, and thistles that littered the ground, and I walked with confidence and was never wounded. I wondered how I was going to be able to walk with shoes on if I couldn't feel what I was walking on.

But there wasn't any time to ponder these questions. My mother was hurrying me to put on the shoes, and she bent down to help me put them on. Then, as if she had read my mind, she added, "We have a long journey ahead."

These sandals were made from car tires, which were inexpensive and easy to obtain. Thin straps wrapped around and under my feet and, passing through the space between my big toe and the one next to it. The unfamiliar feel of the straps rubbing against my foot bothered me, but my curiosity about the evening's strange events easily overwhelmed any thought of the annoying straps. Nogosa was already dressed and went outside to help Abba, who was loading our bags onto the donkey. Migbei slept on, oblivious to all the nighttime activity.

Alofo was dressed, and Ima told us to hold hands and go outside. Hand in hand, we stepped outside, and together we faced the darkness, the silence, and the unknown.

Ima went back inside the house and came out with a small pot cover tied to the straps of the *machzel*, and I realized that we were leaving home permanently so that we could live in far-off Yerushalayim.

Abba lifted Alofo and sat her on the donkey, Nogosa walked on the left side of the donkey, and Abba held the reins from the right side. I held Ima's hand, and we prepared to begin our journey into the unknown, but with a bright destination. Ima explained to us that we

Where Am I Going?

couldn't make any noise. We had to be as quiet as possible, and we couldn't cry or shout.

I saw other signs that we were leaving for good: the ox that was exchanged for a donkey, the frequent mention of Yerushalayim, and the sighs I heard and sadness I saw lingering on people's faces. We were leaving forever, and who knew when I would see our house again, if at all? Even though we were looking ahead to our future, I couldn't help but turn around to look at our house and say good bye in the short time I had left before I wouldn't see it anymore. I looked over at my home and my birthplace, even though I could not see much in the darkness. I saw Savta's and Uncle Chagos' houses, which were situated the closest to our house and were now feeling abandoned. Memories appeared before me like snapshots that I can recreate until today: the special gathering I had attended there when I was three years old, when I first learned about Yerushalayim, the steep hill, the green grass spread out beyond the house, and the Katin Klay River, and remembering them all brought a smile to my face. These were the memories I carried from this house that now stood alone in the darkness. I was suddenly worried about leaving it behind, pitiful and neglected.

Questions started running through my mind one after the other: What would happen to our house? Would somebody else come to live there and fill it with life again, and if someone did come to live there, would they live there the same way we did? I couldn't find any answers in the short time I had left to bid my home farewell, a home that had meant so much to me. Its walls held our joys, our worries, our dreams, and our silence. They held our tears and our prayers, and had even felt the lick of fire when our holy books were burned by Christian marauders. Our house was much like every other house of the Beta Yisrael, built on a foundation of hard work and the dream of one day returning to our Holy Land.

I was four years old when I left, and while only a few memories remain from that time, I can still feel my mother's hand on my back, urging me to turn around and walk a little faster.

We soon met up with another group of people setting out on their own journey, and we joined them. Among those we met were my uncle Legeseh and his family, as well as our uncles Mitzamihret and his brother Birhaneh and their families. Saba Getahun couldn't join us because he was serving in the army, but Savta Adiyeh did. Nine families in all set out into the darkness in complete silence, and I understood that this silence would help us reach Yerushalayim. We had no idea what we were facing—the darkness, the forest, the heat, and the danger—but the words of Tehillim were our prayer: "Let me hear Your kindness at dawn, for in You I have placed my trust; let me know the way I should walk, for to You I have lifted my soul."

When we entered the forest, only the stars lit our way. Ima reminded us that we were going home, and repeated how important it was for us to be quiet.

My mother was amazed at the maturity we exhibited. "You were such little children," she told me many years later, "but you listened to all the instructions we gave you. None of you cried or shouted, and even when you were hungry or thirsty, you didn't ask for food or drink. It was unbelievable!" We all took turns riding on the donkey, and the rest of the time we walked.

"Mitzllal," my mother continued, "you walked for nearly a year on those little feet of yours, until we reached Sudan, and you never took your turn on the donkey. You always let Nogosa or Alofa ride in your place. Nogosa once got down from the donkey so that you could take your turn, but the minute he put his feet down on the ground, he felt tremendous pain in his knee. He bent down, holding his knee in pain, and when you saw how much he was suffering you refused to ride the donkey. 'I can walk!' you insisted. People still remember how brave you were, and even though you were only four years old, you were stronger than others who were much older than you, who were always moaning and complaining. But not you, Mitzllal. You were different."

When the Jewish people came out of Egypt, they wandered in the desert for forty years before they came to Eretz Yisrael. The Beta Yisrael also wandered in the desert for many years amid difficulty and suffering, and their love for Eretz Yisrael only grew stronger in that time. Their strong desire to live in the Land of Our Fathers strengthened them to withstand the pangs of *aliyah*.

So many question marks hovered in the air above us as we traveled. We wondered if we would arrive safely, and if we would be able to bridge the huge gap our isolation from the rest of the Jewish world had formed. But soon the wind came and blew our worries away, as we realized we had nothing to fear. We were going home!

CHAPTER TEN

The First Leg of the Journey

We walked in the forest for close to three hours until we came to the desert. It was two o'clock in the morning, still dark outside, and we pushed our way through rocks, thorns, and dry grass. We walked group by group, with the strongest ones at the head of each group. In our group, Uncle Legeseh's wife, children, and three sons-in-law walked out in front, and Uncle Legeseh followed behind with all the sheep, as he was responsible for shepherding the sheep of all the families. Uncle Mitzamihret, Uncle Birhaneh, and my family came next, since we had small children who walked slowly and had to stop more frequently. Even though we were walking in separate groups, we didn't lose contact with each other. The first group would stop periodically and wait for the other groups to catch up before continuing.

At four o'clock in the morning, we could hear helicopters and shooting off in the distance. At that time, there was a war going on between the Democrats and the Communists, and we could hear the war all the way from where we were, but we kept moving in spite of our fear, our silence surrounding us like a cloak. The only sign of our presence was our footprints in the sand, and we soldiered on even though we were unprepared for the unexpected.

After five straight hours of walking, we were forced to stop. We found ourselves surrounded by a pack of wolves, and the sound of their

The First Leg of the Journey

howling was terrifying. The children, silent up until then, could not contain their cries as they clung to their parents' legs, pulling on their clothing and searching for a place to hide. The children riding on their fathers' shoulders breathed more easily since they were up high and away from the danger. We huddled together, frightened and trembling, until one of the men gathered his courage and threw a lit match into a pile of dried grass. A big fire broke out, scaring the wolves and sending them running for safety.

Before we started moving again, we realized that two donkeys belonging to two families with small children, one of which was ourselves, had disappeared. All of our supplies were loaded on the donkeys, from flour to candies for the children. Without these essential supplies, there was no way we could survive in the desert. They decided to split up: Abba and Uncle Mitzamihret would turn back and look for the donkeys, and the rest of us would continue onward.

We continued walking until the sun came up and we could finally see where we were going. We were alone in the desert—we could neither see the first group ahead of us nor see those who had turned back to find the donkeys—but there was no time to stop because we were in the middle of a war zone.

Later in the morning, Aunt Avishai's labor pains, which she had been enduring for the past ten hours, began to overwhelm her. We knew that we had to stop, but we needed to find a shady spot. Luckily, there was a mountain up ahead that was covered with trees. When we got there, Uncle Birhaneh cleared away stones and branches and starting breaking branches off trees, with my mother helping as much as she could. We laid the branches on the ground and spread blankets over them. We tied three of the blankets to four trees surrounding the clearing to set up a partition of sorts where Avishai, after giving birth, would be able to rest with her baby. The children were exhausted and fell asleep right away. Aunt Avishai approached the partition from the other side with Aunt Yejevnesh accompanying. Aunt Yejevnesh was carrying Avishai's toddler on her back and holding Avishai's hand, trying to comfort her.

Aunt Avishai went inside the partition, and everyone waited to hear good news. Avishai was in tremendous pain, and Aunt Yejevnesh was telling her what she could do to minimize the pain. After a few long and nerve-wracking minutes, we could hear a baby's cry.

"Mazel tov!" said Aunt Yejevnesh. "It's an adorable baby girl." It was also a ray of light in the gathering gloom.

The new mother did not have much time to rest and recover. We started walking only two hours after the birth, with Avishai holding her new baby and her midwife carrying the baby's two-year-old sister.

We continued walking for a few more hours, and while we were walking, we saw two of Uncle Legeseh's sons-in-law who had turned back to find out what had happened to us. We filled them in on the reason for our delay, and it was decided, following a brief discussion, that we would wait for my father and Uncle Mitzamihret to return from their search for the donkeys. Meanwhile, we realized that Uncle Legeseh had vanished along with the sheep. Twelve hours had passed with no word of his whereabouts, and his family, who had already crossed the Tekezeh River, turned back and waited for their father to appear.

While we were waiting, we heard cows lowing, and a little while later, Uncle Legeseh's third son-in-law appeared, followed shortly by my father and Uncle Mitzamihret, whole and unharmed. They told us they were caught by armed soldiers who called themselves "Machber Minasai." Describing themselves as "affiliated with the Democrats," they interrogated my father and uncle for hours, from morning until

The First Leg of the Journey

four o'clock in the afternoon. Only after explaining that they were wandering farmers looking to find work did the soldiers let them go. Uncle Legeseh had also been caught by the soldiers, and they let him go after he convinced them that he was a simple shepherd.

Just after breathing a sigh of relief, we realized that Abba and Uncle Mitzamihret had come back empty-handed—without donkeys, flour, or water. The families with small children were left without food and water, but we told my father and Uncle Mitzamihret the good news about Avishai's baby, and they were consoled.

We tried to see the good in the situation—we were all together, everyone had returned in one piece, and a new baby had joined our group.

We continued our journey. Uncle Legeseh joined up with his family, and we all followed the two young men who had waited for us to come, because they already knew the way. When we came to the great Tekezeh River, however, we had no idea how to cross it with little children in our care.

Uncle Mitzamihret held a long stick in his hand and stood close to the mouth of the river. Everyone was frozen in place, wondering whether it was feasible to achieve this seemingly impossible task. This particular scenario of a man waving his hand over the water was well known to those among us who learned Torah.

One hundred and twenty years earlier, a large group of people attempted to travel from Ethiopia to Yerushalayim. At their head was Abba Mahari, a man in pursuit of a dream he'd had. In this dream, Hashem revealed to him that it was time for him to go up to Yerushalayim. He abandoned his homeland, and many others joined the expedition. When they got to the river, he spread his staff over it, expecting the same miracle as that that occurred by the Yam Suf.

Unfortunately, the river did not split, and Abba Mahari and his retinue were forced to return home. Many of them never reached home, having fallen on the way from sickness and plagues. This failed attempt ended in bitter disappointment.

This time, Uncle Mitzamihret did not put his faith in miracles and expect the river to split. With the water coming up to his chest, he crossed the river with his staff in one hand and a child in the other. Each man did the same, and before they knew it, all the children were safely on the other side. Then they held the women by their hands and crossed them over, as well. We were soaked to the marrow of our bones but thrilled with our success.

Still soaking wet, we had to pass through tall grass that was nearly a meter (approximately three feet) high.

After a few hours, the grassy part ended, and we came upon a clearing where we met up with the first group. They had spread out blankets and had already fallen asleep. We were happy that we, too, could finally rest, and we started to unload our things and get ready to sleep. It was one o'clock on a Friday morning.

Abba lowered Alofo from his shoulders, and like all the other fathers, spread a blanket on the ground. My brother and I were awake but exhausted. Ima changed us into the dry clothing she had carried on her shoulder along with the *machzel* that held my baby sister. She spread the wet clothing out to dry, and then she put the four of us to sleep on the blanket spread out on the ground and covered us with another blanket. Ima looked at us and started to cry. It pained her to see us sleeping on a blanket on the ground like that, but it hurt even more when she considered our situation.

"I'll never forget it as long as I live," my mother later told me. "I lifted my hands up to Shamayim and prayed from the bottom of my heart: 'Master of the World,' I cried. 'You know that my mother is ill, that she has been paralyzed for the past nine years, and that my brother Kakhsai has been sitting in prison for months and I have no idea what will happen to him. I didn't want to leave my mother and my brother behind, but the people in our village convinced us that the time had come to go to Yerushalayim. We got up and left, leaving behind my mother and brother so that I could fulfill the dream of thousands of years, *and here is my sacrifice!*'

"I pointed my finger at you children lying so helplessly before me and said, 'Master of the World, look at these children, walking for hours at a time without making a cry or complaint. The last meal they ate was the night before we left, and it's been a whole day since they've eaten. It's one o'clock in the morning now, and another day is dawning. What will I give my children to eat and drink? We have no flour! We have no water! Their last meal satisfied them until now, but what about the next day? I can't even think about it, but in spite of it all, I still want to go to Yerushalayim with my children.'" My mother placed her hands over her eyes, wiped her tears with them, and kissed them, as was her custom when she finished praying.

Aunt Yejevnesh, sitting a short distance away with Aunt Avishai, overheard my mother's prayer and rebuked her soundly. "Why are you crying that you have no flour or water? Why are you worrying? We are all here together. We'll eat whatever there is, and if we'll finish it all, we'll all fast together. Here, take this flour and water from us, and make bread for everyone." Ima cried again, only this time from joy.

Ima set out her supplies and quickly prepared the dough while Abba broke up some branches into kindling. Ima hesitated for a moment, regretting the absence of her baking pan, when she remembered that she had tied a pot cover onto one of the straps of the baby carrier because there hadn't been room for it anywhere else. Ima spread out the dough on top of the pot cover and set it to bake, and that was how we ate our bread, called *kicha*, in the middle of the forest. Ima also made *intatiyeh*, chick pea flour mixed with water, which we spread on the *kicha* before folding it back in half. The children were woken up for a taste and then fell back asleep.

Ima continued baking until about four in the morning. The first group, Uncle Legeseh and his family, ate some of the fresh bread before embarking on the next part of the journey. They arranged a time and place for the next rendezvous and went on their way. Ima, much more relaxed knowing her children had food to eat, finally went to sleep.

It's hard to fathom how anyone could have slept at all under these conditions. Any one of them—the war, the forbidding forest, the wild animals, the robbers, and the exhaustion—would have stopped others with less faith in G-d. The words of *Tefillat Haderech*, the prayer for travelers, came to life as we prayed for safety, "You should lead us in peace, lay us down in peace, and direct our steps in peace so that we should arrive at our destination in peace!"

And so it was. We saw with our own eyes how Hashem guided us on every step of the grueling journey. We looked directly into the faces of wild animals, and we weren't harmed. We stepped into the path of robbers, armed soldiers, and policemen and emerged unscathed. We believed in Hashem and knew He would protect us, and with this calm, we fell asleep.

Because it had been dark when we arrived, we had no idea what an idyllic setting we had wandered into. We awoke at three o'clock in the afternoon that Friday and looked around us in wonder. We were surrounded by green pastures, where our cattle grazed contentedly, and the trees were so tall and abundant that their branches were joined together above us to form a canopy over our heads.

CHAPTER ELEVEN

Nowhere to Go

By now we had crossed over towering mountain ranges under a broiling sun, and the group was sighing for lack of water. All of us, from the youngest to the oldest, traipsed forward in a long procession as we slowly made our way onward. The silence was deafening, the only sounds far off and frightening. We had no idea where we were going; there were no trails in the desert, no flashlights or signposts. We had only our will and our faith to guide us.

After three weeks of travel, we reached the village of Mezega. We learned from the local Jews there, who had also tried to reach Eretz Yisrael, that our arduous journey had been for nothing. There was no way into Sudan and no way out of Sudan to Eretz Yisrael. We fell into a state of shock upon hearing this news. After some deliberation, we realized there was no choice but to turn back.

With heavy hearts, we retraced our footsteps. As soon as we started out, we were accosted by two soldiers whose appearance terrified us. We had already learned to identify the Democratic and Communist soldiers we encountered along the way, but we didn't recognize these two. Their uniforms were different, and they were carrying large and powerful weapons. They interrogated us for a few hours, and after we answered their questions to their satisfaction, they told us they knew the whereabouts of the two donkeys we had lost. They explained that they were affiliated with the Democrats, and they had given the donkeys to them as a gesture of good faith, but the load wasn't nearly as heavy as they thought it would be. He then added, "If you are telling us the truth, give us all your money so the commander will believe us when we tell him that you are being honest, and then we can let you go. If he sees that you have money, he will think that you are liars and your end at his hand will not be a pleasant one."

One of my uncles immediately handed over the sixty thousand birr (about $3,000) he had in his possession to the soldier, who was apparently satisfied because he didn't ask anyone else for money. They did, however, relieve us of the *khoada* (a pure silver canteen that held three liters of hard butter) and a *karah* (knife), saying they needed to show them to their commander. They asked us if there were other groups coming up behind us, and when we told him there were, they started walking in the direction they would be coming from. The uncle who had given them the money shouted, "Should we wait for you here?" in the hopes that he would get his money back. The soldiers called back that we should wait for them and went on their way. My father realized that we had been swindled and said, "They are thieves, Uncle. You won't be seeing your money again. Let's get out of here quickly."

It took three weeks of walking until we returned home. Once again, we crossed the Tekezeh River through the forest and walked along its side by way of the cornfield. When we arrived at our village, we were greeted with shouts of welcome from our neighbors, but our homes had been completely ransacked and emptied of our possessions while we were gone.

The non-Jews had helped themselves to all of our good clothing, scattering the rest all over the floor, as well as our spices, bowls, and pitchers. They had even ripped off the cloth coverings from our beds. Our beautiful and orderly room had been reduced to rubble, and it appeared even smaller than it had before.

We cleaned up as best we could, spreading blankets on the floor so we could sleep. We had a lot of work in front of us; we needed to restore our home and adjust to being back.

When our neighbors, the Muslims and Christians, saw us, they feigned anger. "Why did you run away from us?" they asked. "Aren't we good enough for you?" However, at the same time, they agreed to return only the flour and spices from the items they had taken, and even that, only on condition that we give them something in return. Some of the Jewish women had handmade clay pitchers that they gave to the non-Jews in exchange for the spices. Ima could now return the flour she had borrowed from Aunt Yejevnesh.

CHAPTER TWELVE

The Second Attempt

A month after our disappointing return, we were informed that it was now permitted to enter Sudan. Once again, we gathered all of our things and arranged a day and time for departure. This time, we sold all of our sheep and left in the light of day, and not like thieves in the night as we had before. We also received a pass from the head of the Democratic regime. They knew we had already tried to leave Ethiopia once before, and realizing that it was going to be impossible to stop us, decided to let us go.

The path was familiar to us now: the cornfield, the meadow, the river. We were once again swallowed up by the forest and once again crossed mountains and valleys, some of which were covered with trees and others which were barren. Some of the paths were treacherous, dust and rocks forcing us to walk slowly and carefully, and others were winding and led from one mountain to the next. We met many people along the way who were making the same journey.

My parents had also decided that Savta Indaya and her family would be joining us this time. Ima insisted, "I need my mother with us this time."

As we neared the city of Asgedeh, the home of my father's sister Tivletz (though we children called her "Aunt Amuyeh"), he split off from the group to buy a horse there. The horse he chose was big and strong, dark brown with a beautiful coat. He then set out on his horse to Adiabo to gather Savta Indaya and her family.

The Second Attempt

Abba had already heard from fellow travelers that the Communists had invaded Adi Abu and that everyone had fled, except for Savta Indaya, who could not walk. He later learned that all he'd heard was true, that the Dergi (Communists) had indeed attacked the village, causing widespread panic. Jews, Christians, and Muslims alike had run for their lives, scattering in every direction. Aunt Maisu had run in one direction, and her children ran in another, leaving Savta Indaya alone. For three days, the village lay abandoned with no one there besides for Savta Indaya. Seeing the door of her home flung wide open, some soldiers stepped in to see what they could find and found Savta Indaya sitting on her bed, terrified. She explained to the soldiers that she was ill and couldn't walk, and they tried to reassure her. "Don't be afraid! We aren't going to hurt you!" The soldiers helped themselves to a flask of honey and a flask of sour cream, sat down and ate, and then went on their way.

Abba arrived at Adiabo on Sunday. As he approached the entrance to the city, he noticed members of the Communist regime riding back and forth on their horses, but not entering. When the coast was clear, Abba entered the village undetected. He noticed all the abandoned houses, but he continued onward to Savta's house, where he found her terrified and in tears. Aunt Maisu and her children returned later in the afternoon, along with some others from the village, once they saw that the danger had passed. Abba stayed for three or four days, helping Aunt Maisu sell her possessions, until he finally announced, "Savta, it's time to go! I will help you. Everyone is waiting."

Savta burst into bitter tears. "I can't go!" she cried. She had wished for this day for so long, but the timing just wasn't right. She couldn't leave without her son, Kakhsai, who was still sitting in jail. "I can't go," she said again, and burst into tears once more. "I'm staying here!

You go. I will manage; don't worry about me. I will wait until the time is right!"

Aunt Maisu and her family were already waiting outside. When she saw that Abba was delayed, she went inside to see what was wrong. "Come, Ima, everyone is waiting. Let's go," she said, but Savta's tears were heartbreaking.

"I can't go without my son," she said. "I will wait for Kakhsai. Please, go on ahead, I will be fine here. I'll wait for him, and we will meet you there. Please, leave me!" she cried, holding on tightly to both sides of her bed.

Aunt Meisu tried again to convince her to leave. "Ima, you must come! This is the time. Don't worry, Kakhsai will join us. Please, come with us!"

But Savta wouldn't budge. "I'm not going without my son, and that's final." Her Muslim neighbors heard her cries, and they, too, tried to convince her to travel with her family. They then told Abba and my aunt that they had better go before it was too late, and that they would take care of Savta. They'd give her water to drink and some flour so she could make food for herself.

Abba and Aunt Maisu had no idea what to do. How could they leave Savta in the hands of these Muslims? Left with no other choice, they agreed to take Savta against her will. They pulled her fingers from the bed she had been grasping and Abba lifted her up and sat her on the horse he had just purchased. One of the Christians sat by her side, hired by my father to accompany us to Sudan and help Savta. He received the first payment at the outset, and he would receive the rest upon arrival in Sudan, where they would part company. Savta continued to weep, crying "Kakhsai, my son! What will become of you?" Her mother's heart refused to part from him.

The Second Attempt

With eyes reddened by tears and constant lament for her son on her lips, Savta arrived on horseback to Asgede, accompanied by Abba and Maisu and her family. She continued to murmur these words without cease for the rest of the journey, her feelings of guilt unabated, even for a moment. She never forgave herself for leaving her son behind. Her mother's heart never healed from the pain and accompanied her until her last day.

In the forest near the entrance to Asgedeh, we met up with Abba and the rest of the family. Other Jews, also on their way to Sudan, joined up with us, including five *kayasim* (religious leaders) with their families. They brought the number of travelers in our group up to 123. Eight men, non-Jews, had offered their services as guides, citing the names of all the people they had accompanied to Sudan. The people they mentioned happened to have been related to us, and we knew for a fact that they had indeed arrived safely in Sudan, so we trusted them. Their leader, Setay, was the oldest of them; the rest were young men.

They took their places at the front of our group, spreading out in all directions, and we walked silently behind them. After two hours of walking, Setay and his men stopped for a whispered consultation. After they had finished talking, Setay approached us, informing us of their decision. "Listen," he said. "We have walked with you and have shown you which way to go, but we are facing great danger if we are caught with you. We will be punished severely, so we must insist that you give us more money than the amount we had originally agreed on." He named the sum, then said, "If you don't give us more money now, we won't be able to continue guiding you."

"We trusted them," my mother told me. Each family took from their money until we had enough to pay them, after which they thanked us and we continued walking onward.

After another two hours, the same story repeated itself, and then it happened five more times after that. The sixth time, they didn't bother asking us for more money; they simply went looking for it themselves. We had just sat down to drink coffee and eat matzah when an argument broke out between Setay and his men. The youths were certain that we were hiding our money from them in our sacks of flour, and they wanted to spill the sacks and look for it, but Setay pretended to violently disagree. "If you touch their flour, I will kill you."

Setay shouted at them, holding his ground and pressing his finger on the trigger of his weapon. The youths paid no attention to him and made a beeline for the flour. The women begged Setay to stop the fighting. "Please don't fight them; just let them spill the flour!" They agreed to whatever it would take to stop the fight. They were afraid that if the men would start shooting at each other, we would get caught in the crossfire.

One of the men approached Setay with a cup of coffee and a piece of *kicha* in his hand, trying to calm him down. "Setay, here, have a drink," he said. "Don't get so angry."

But Setay was too wound up to drink. "How can I drink this hot coffee when I myself am boiling over with rage?" While we were attempting to calm him down, we could see a group of fearsome men approaching, but we didn't pay any attention to them. We were too busy worrying about what was happening in front of us.

After an hour's rest, Setay eventually drank the coffee, but he was still angry. Once again, the men spoke among themselves, and before long, two of Setay's group broke off and returned a short while later with another group of men. Their hair was long and grey, pulled upward and held in place by a *mido*, a hand-shaped comb that was used to part the hair and braid it. Setay and his men explained that these men would be our night watchmen, and they settled down on the ground we had prepared for sleeping. The truth was that they had asked this group of men to watch us so we wouldn't run off with our money.

This fearsome-looking group sang throughout the whole night, and when they'd take a break from singing, they'd shout, "Bring us your girls!" We were terrified. We didn't know what to do, and the girls were beside themselves. We gathered our courage and shouted back, "We have no girls! We are all married! This woman is married to that man, and that man is married to that woman!" We "married" girls to their brothers, uncles to aunts, pointing out each one until there was not one girl left "unmarried." The hooligans miraculously believed us and continued singing. This time, everything ended well, but there were other times when the outcome was tragic.

"They kept on singing," my mother later told me, "and we didn't have a moment of peace. We didn't sleep a wink and prayed that nothing bad would happen to us, *chalilah*. They finally stopped their singing in the morning when Setay and his men returned, refreshed and ready to continue with the journey. The fearsome band went their own way, to our great relief. We drank some coffee, hoping that it would energize us, ate matzah, and once again shouldered our burdens and set out.

We followed Setay and his men through the desert for two hours. As we prepared to climb the high dunes, we saw no living thing with the exception of an army of ants. Setay and his men showed us how to climb and told us that when we'd reach the other side, we'd see a well and a tall tree beside it. "Put your things down beside the tree," they said, "and wait for us there."

We were happy to hear that we would be stopping in the shade, with a well no less, and we started to climb. We couldn't have imagined the trap these evil men had set for us. We reached the tree on the other side of the mountain and started to unload our things when we saw our "night watchmen" approaching us once again. We weren't afraid of them the day before, when we were with Setay and his men, but this time we didn't have anyone with us. Our terror grew as they came closer, and we could see that they were carrying weapons in their hands; some had axes, and others had heavy branches and metal rods.

Suddenly, we heard a volley of shots and shouting coming from the other side of the mountain. We threw ourselves on the ground, covering our heads with our hands. The smaller children were cowering beneath their parents. Setay and his men had planned to ambush us so they could help themselves to the rest of our money, and they had joined forces with the bandits, promising them part of the spoils if they would help them. They beat the men mercilessly, demanding them to give them their money. When they got to Kayas Goyaitai, they stopped short. Kayas Goyaitai stood tall and straight as a tree, his entire being radiating honor and glory, holding his most precious possession: a *sefer Torah* written in Urit, a Gez dialect, that was protected for many years and was still being learned and taught. The bandit gestured to Kayas Goyaitai to hand it over, assuming there was money hidden inside. Kayas Goyaitai at first held on to it tightly, but was forced to capitulate to the bandit's demand. Suddenly, the bandit screamed, holding out his bloodied right hand. Petrified, he quickly returned the terrifying object to Kayas Goyaitai, unaware that he had hidden a sharp knife in the *sefer Torah* and that it was this that had wounded him.

The non-Jew Abba had hired to accompany my grandmother intervened then, hoping to calm things down. "When I was your age, I did the same thing as you are doing now," he said. "Only I, unlike you, only took money. I didn't eat the flesh of my victims, nor did I drink their blood."

As soon as he finished speaking, one of the bandits lifted up his axe and moved toward Savta's guard. "You think you're such a hero?"

he said to the guard. "Go and bring the old woman water before she faints!" He rushed to bring water to Savta, who indeed looked like she was about to faint. Savta drank the water and started to look a bit better.

After it had quieted down some, the members of our group looked around to make sure their loved ones were all accounted for, and we realized that Mosfun, a seven-year-old boy, was missing. He had run away to escape the turmoil, with no idea where he was going, his only thought to get as far away as he could. Everyone set out to look for him until he was spotted on the top of a mountain. He looked like a little star shining over the tall mountain. His mother fainted when she realized how far he had gotten and how high he had climbed. Her children started to scream, "Ima! Ima!" They threw water on her, watching over her while Setay and his men went out to rescue the boy and bring him back to his mother.

She returned to normal when her son returned, but our own fears allowed us no rest: What would happen now? What would be with us?

Suddenly, without warning, a thick fog settled over us. It was so thick we couldn't see each other. The moment it lifted, Setay and his men parted from us, saying that from now on we would be guided by another group of men. They conferred among themselves, and then Setay and his men left. We were now being led by four men brandishing spears and axes.

We were starting to climb a particularly slippery slope when one of the horses slipped and threw off the seven-year-old girl who was riding him. When her father tried to pick her up, he saw that her head was lolling from side to side and falling backward without support. It was a terrifying sight, and members of our group began to scream. Her father tried to revive her, but the water spilled out of her mouth when he gave her to drink. Her eyes were closed. When we started to cry, the guides began to yell, "Shut up, you disgusting Jews. What are you crying about? If she is dead, then go bury her and quit your crying." His words reminded us that death was not an unusual occurrence on these journeys from Ethiopia to Sudan. Many travelers lost their lives along the way. The girl's father lifted her up and held her in his arms, walking with her that way until we stopped to rest. After a while, the girl recovered from her fall, but for a long time afterward we wouldn't forget the sight of her being unconscious.

The sun was just about to set. We stood atop a mountain covered with dry grass that was as tall as a man. It sounded like snapping branches when we walked over it. The guides told us to stop where we were and put our things down. Savta's guide lifted her down from her horse and set the horse free. He knew what we didn't, that the guides were about to strip us of the rest of our possessions. These thieves in disguise chose three of our horses, and when they saw the fourth had escaped, they chose another one in its place. Then they turned their attention to our possessions, helping themselves to the nicest of our clothing and utensils: the *jebena* (coffee pot), foodstuffs, shoes, jewelry, and they even took the jerry can we kept filled with water. My mother panicked because she had hidden a pair of gold earrings wrapped in cloth at the bottom of the jerry can, and she was terrified they would find it and punish her. At the last minute, one of the four thieves decided to let us keep the jerry can so that we should at least have what to drink. My mother heaved a sigh of relief, grateful that both she and the earrings were safe.

After they had taken what they wanted, they finally turned back and left the way they came. It was nine o'clock at night, and complete darkness closed in around us. Surrounded by the tall grass, we stood without moving the entire night. We were at the top of the mountain, and below us we were surrounded by a ring of fire. The danger was palpable, and all we could do was cry and pray. The adults lifted their hands and kissed them as they prayed, and the children held on to them, imitating their gestures. There we stood until morning came, begging the *Ribono Shel Olam* to save us.

At six thirty in the morning, we could clearly see the remains of the fire that had threatened us, and we realized that a miracle had been performed for us. We ate a breakfast of coffee and bread and prepared to move on, though we didn't know what the future held. Where were we supposed to go from there? Who was going to guide us and show us the way to Sudan? We did not know the answers, we only knew that we at least had to try. Three men went ahead to search for the trail, and when they came back, they were murmuring words of thanks for Hashem's salvation. Until we set out, we had no way of knowing that we were right at the edge of a deep chasm. If we had taken one more step forward in the darkness, we would have been lost to its depths.

We climbed up the side of a mountain, which was the equivalent of walking straight up a slanted wall with no foot- or handholds to cling to. My mother later commented how surprised she had been that the horses didn't fall backward. Following this treacherous ascent was an equally dangerous descent that almost sent us tumbling.

We had just made our way down carefully and had found ourselves in the desert once again when we saw a man riding on a donkey off in the distance. He looked simple and not at all threatening, unlike those two-faced bandits we had encountered earlier. We rejoiced at the sight of him. When he approached us, we greeted him and he greeted us back, and then we asked him where he was coming from.

"Yesterday," he told us, "I wanted to return home when I suddenly heard shooting. I was very frightened. I met a group of people who recommended that I turn back because they had seen a group of people—men, women, and children—who'd been battered and beaten. I listened to them and turned back, stopping to sleep at Adi Keyikh. And you?" he asked. "Where are you going? Are you the group I heard about yesterday?" We told him we were, and then asked him where we were and in which direction Sudan was located. He replied that we were about two hours away from Adi Keyikh. From there, we'd be able to continue onward and ask for additional directions along the way.

We parted from the man and continued to walk, each one lost in his own thoughts of Yerushalayim. We had assumed, according to Parda Aklum's account, that the journey to Eretz Yisrael was only a matter of days, but we soon discovered that the journey was long and arduous, filled with obstacles along the way.

"Yerushalayim of Gold, Yerushalayim of Light," we prayed. "Please illuminate our way to you. We only want to come to you! Where are you, Yerushalayim? Where are you?"

CHAPTER THIRTEEN

Searching for Help

After two more hours of walking, the scenery around us began to change from a desert beige to a lively green. We passed grassy fields, shady fruit trees, and a flowing river. We could see young shepherds and their flocks off in the distance near the village. We felt the Hand of Hashem watching over us and blessing our arrival. The crowing roosters reminded us of the homes we'd left behind.

We stopped to rest near a well some distance from the village. We unloaded our things and sat down, stretching our aching feet on the soft grass. The children who were being carried by donkeys or shouldered by their parents were happy to touch the ground again. We were tired, hungry, thirsty, and aching. We drank our fill from the well, and then washed our hands and faces in the hopes that the cool water would wash away our pangs of aches and hunger. The water revived us, giving us newfound energy to move on. Our long and tedious journey through the desert heightened our appreciation for the fruit trees and their blessed shade. We decided to remain where we were and spend Shabbat there.

We were so busy with our many tasks that we did not notice the group of people coming toward us from the village. At their head was a Communist soldier who asked us, "Where did you come from, and where are you going?"

"We are on our way to Chomora," we answered. "The war in

Ethiopia has made life very difficult for us. We thought that we would go to Chomora until the situation was more stable and then later return home and support our families properly."

The soldier seemed to accept our response, but then he began counting us from youngest to oldest and wrote our names down in a little notebook he pulled out from his pocket.

After completing his count, he instructed us to relocate our camp to a spot nearer to the village. With little choice, we complied and moved all of our things to the place he pointed out to us.

We soon became occupied with regular activities. Women were nursing their babies, feeding the children, and making coffee on makeshift ovens. Ground *boon* (coffee) was put to boil, and as the coffee was poured out into cups, the rich aroma filled the air. My father was grazing the sheep at a distance from where we were camped, and after a while, my mother began wondering why he wasn't back yet.

She later told me, "When I saw that Abba was late coming back, I got angry with my two nieces, Tzahainesh and Zigvah, who were eleven or twelve at that time. 'Why didn't you go and take care of the sheep?' I scolded them. 'You children had a chance to eat, but I never drink coffee without my husband.' Tzahainesh and Zigvah were terribly embarrassed by my outburst. I waited and waited for him to come back, and I couldn't fathom why he wasn't coming yet. Suddenly, I heard someone shout, 'He left his wife and children behind and ran off!'

"'How can that be?' I asked myself, shocked. 'Is it true?' Shaken to the core, I began to weep. One of the women sitting near me leaned over and whispered, 'Don't worry, you're with us. We'll help you with everything.' But my pain was too great for me to bear. I refused to believe that this could be happening. Abba had simply left the sheep where they were and had run away."

Searching for Help

Meanwhile, the uniformed soldier, after a brief consultation with his men, returned to our group. He read all our names out once again and soon discovered that two of the men were missing. We replied immediately that no one was missing and that there must be a mistake. The soldier didn't believe us. He circled the names of the missing men and warned us that whoever tried to escape would be severely punished. "Tomorrow, we will take you wherever you want to go, to Sudan or Chomora," he added. They had no intention of doing that; they only said it to keep us calm and cooperative.

It was already late Friday afternoon, so we told him that we couldn't go anywhere on Shabbat. "We'll take you on Sunday, then," he said.

When I grew older, I very much wanted to know what had caused my father to run away the way he did, but Abba never wanted to talk about it. One day, after we pleaded with him for a long time, did he agree to tell us what happened, even though it was very difficult for him.

"I knew that Shabbat was just about to start, and I knew that it was forbidden to walk so far on Shabbat, but I thought that our situation fell into the category of *pikuach nefesh*, a matter of life and death," he told us. "My intention was to go and get help from the Democrats, and I assured myself that Hashem would forgive me. 'Shabbos Queen, forgive me and watch over me,' I said, and then I slipped away and ran off." Until today, Abba still feels terribly guilty over what he did.

I sat across from my father and listened to his story. It was the first time he had ever spoken about it; he had kept it buried inside of him all this time. "Please don't write about this in your book," he said when he saw that I was taking notes. I pretended that I didn't understand and asked why I shouldn't. Abba replied, "I failed! I couldn't find anyone to help us. I was hoping I would find help right away. I imagined myself returning with a group of soldiers and rescuing everyone, but it just never happened. For four months, I was away from my family. My little children, who had always seen me as their protector, now realized that their father was gone."

I saw the pain on my father's face and I hurt along with him. Trying to comfort him, I said, "This is exactly the kind of thing I should write about—the courage and strength you displayed. You risked your life for us. From the moment you left us, you spent all of your energy in trying to rescue us. You were so brave, and in the end, you did find help. You didn't rest for a moment until you could come back to get us. When the time was right, you crossed back from Sudan to Ethiopia and smuggled us over the border. You planned everything out. We crossed over group by group, and right after the fourth and last group had arrived safely, you were caught.

"It was more painful for me to see you caught than it was during the entire time you were away. After all you had gone through to get all of us out of Ethiopia, you were caught and beaten in front of all the people you had saved. The Sudanese soldiers beat you mercilessly, and you still carry the scars from their whips. The pain in your knees you feel today came from those beatings. Don't feel guilty, Abba. You never stopped being the head of our family. You protected us then, and you still protect us now. You did the right thing, and you were so brave. We need to write about your courage and strength so that everyone will read about the courageous Jews of Ethiopia. And you, Abba, are living proof of it!"

When I finished speaking, my father's eyes lifted and met mine, but now they looked different. The tears were gone, and they were glowing. Abba understood what I was saying and agreed to let me tell his story.

After he'd slipped away from the others tending the sheep, he started running as fast as he could. As he glanced quickly over his shoulder, he

Searching for Help

saw that there was someone following him. Terrified, he careened off the trail, lost himself in the forest, and climbed one of the trees. He sat there, silent and shaking from fear. *If they catch me, I'm finished!* he thought. He closed his eyes for a moment, asking forgiveness from his Creator and saying *Vidui*, in case these were his final moments.

When he opened his eyes, there was utter silence. Abba looked around, hoping to catch a glimpse of whoever had been running after him, but there was no sign of him. Abba climbed down from the tree slowly and walked through the forest for eight more hours without stopping. It was 1:00 a.m. His feet were throbbing, and he was completely exhausted. But how could he sleep? Where could he sleep? He thought of climbing a tree, but feared that if he'd fall asleep and fall to the ground, he would be consumed by a wild animal or killed by pursuing soldiers. As he decided to continue walking, a fire burning on one of the mountains nearby caught his eye. When he got closer and heard cows and sheep, Abba thought there were probably shepherds there who were most likely harmless. He saw two men drinking milk by the fire with two dogs at their sides, confirming his assumption.

He went over to talk to them, and they asked him where he was from and where he was going. "I'm from Tigrei," he answered. "I'm on my way to Sudan."

"What are you doing here at this hour?" they asked.

"I'm looking for my horse. I paid a lot of money for it and it ran away from me."

The shepherds invited Abba to warm up by the fire, and they gave him some warm milk to drink. Abba drank it while the others went to milk the cow for more milk. Abba stretched out, and as soon as he rested his head on his arms, he fell asleep. One of the men shook him awake and gave him another cup of milk. "You must be exhausted," he said. Abba realized that he had no other choice but to sleep.

In the morning, Abba asked the men how to get to Chandayit (in Sudan), and they pointed him in the right direction. He thanked them and left.

It was Shabbat morning when Abba reached Chandayit, and he went looking for Democratic soldiers. To his surprise, he encountered a very familiar face: Daniel, the other man from their group who had gone missing. "How did you manage to get here?" asked Abba. "Where is the rest of the group?"

"I followed you," Daniel replied. "I don't know where they are."

Only then did Abba realize who had been running behind him in the forest.

CHAPTER FOURTEEN

Imprisoned in Chomora

Abba and Daniel decided to appeal to the Democrats for help. They asked around about their location and made their way there in hopes of receiving their assistance. When they arrived, they met with the soldier in charge. The Democratic soldiers found it hard to believe their story and decided to assist them, but at their own pace. They told Abba and Daniel that they would send someone ahead to verify their story, which they did. In the end, though, the messenger was so late in returning that the soldiers decided to go with Abba and Daniel to see what was happening with their own eyes.

Forty soldiers accompanied Abba and Daniel, and along the way, they met the messenger they had sent ahead disguised as a beggar dressed in rags. "I saw a group of people," he reported. "Women, children, and a flock of sheep. They were surrounded by Communist soldiers who were arguing over what to do with their captives. Some said they should bring them to Sudan, and others were saying they should imprison them in Chomora. The strange thing was that the Communist soldier in charge was a double agent, working also as a soldier for the Democrats."

The soldiers gave a signed letter to my father and Daniel commanding the Communist soldiers to release the captives and let them continue walking to Sudan. Abba and Daniel took the letter happily and headed toward Adi Keyikh, parting amicably with the soldiers who went back the way they came.

When Abba and Daniel reached the spot from where they had originally separated from the group, it was Sunday morning, and they didn't see us there. They continued walking, asking anyone they met if they had passed a group of people along the way. One of them replied that they had indeed seen a group surrounded by soldiers who were saying, "We will take them to the Chomora prison in Ethiopia."

Abba listened to their report and said, "We have a letter signed by Democratic soldiers demanding they release the group to Sudan. Maybe we can still reach them before they take them to prison."

The travelers hurried to correct Abba's mistaken assumptions. "Do you think you can give the Communists a letter from their enemy and remain alive? If you value your life, turn around and save yourselves." With that, they left and went on their way.

Abba and Daniel didn't know what to do, so they decided to keep going until they found us. When they finally caught up with us, they saw the soldiers surrounding us from every direction. Abba wavered between taking a chance and delivering the letter from the Democrats in the hopes that we would be saved, or taking the advice from the strangers and turning back. Deep down, they knew the strangers were right; if they would deliver the letter, they would most likely meet their end, so they dodged the soldiers and ran off, determined to find another way to help us. Before he left, Abba caught sight of the two trucks that had come to take us away. We boarded the trucks and were taken to Adi Gosho in Ethiopia, where we slept out in the open for two weeks. Abba and Daniel turned back with the letter in their hands and regret in their hearts.

Two weeks later, we were taken to the Chomora prison. It consisted

Imprisoned in Chomora

of a small open area with two entrances, guarded by six policemen each. A very high fence surrounded the area, and there was a glass barrier on top of the fence supported by concrete. There were neither cells there nor beds, just dirt and rocks. We were forced to sleep on the ground, but this time, there was not even any grass to cushion our bodies.

The only opportunity we had to leave the prison and feel like human beings again was when we were taken to the river to bathe. We were escorted there by twelve guards and then ordered to bathe. We all stood there and stared at the water. "Whoever wants to bathe, do it now!" the guard bellowed. How were we supposed to bathe like that, everyone together, without compromising our modesty? Again we heard shouts behind us, so we went into the water—men, women, and children—with our clothes on. The guards burst out laughing, then quickly announced that our time was up. We wrung out our clothing and returned to the prison, the dirt, and the filth.

At the same time, Abba and Daniel, who were by now in Sudan, met a group of Jews who suggested they break us out of the prison. Abba and Daniel took their advice and crossed back over from Sudan to Ethiopia. As they neared the prison, they could see us from a distance, but they also saw the six guards at each entrance and the high fence that was impossible to cross. They sat there for three days, waiting for a break in the scrutiny of the guards or any other chance to rescue us. Their anguish deepened when they saw that there was no way to rescue even one of us under such tight security. On the third day, two trucks came again and transferred us to Gondar. Abba and Daniel returned to Chandayit in Sudan and continued to search for a solution.

We spent an entire month in the Chomora prison before we went to Gondar, while Abba and Daniel increased their efforts to free us. They decided to appeal to the Israeli delegates in Gedarif to help us gain our freedom. They left Chandayit in the middle of the night and walked to the outskirts of the city. They stood on the main road and waited for someone to drive by and pick them up. After a short while, a truck stopped. "Are you running from the Red Cross?" the driver asked, smiling at them. "For the right price, I can take you wherever you want to go." They settled on an amount, and Abba and Daniel got in the truck, asking him to let them off at Wadi al Chilo. They contacted the Red Cross, who arranged a place for them to stay. In the middle of the night, they went out again and were picked up by another truck driver. They got off in Gedarif and met up with Ethiopian agents who were appointed by the Israeli government to help Ethiopian Jews emigrate to Eretz Yisrael.

There were a lot of refugees waiting their turn in Gedarif. Whenever new refugees arrived, the agents directed them to the right place to receive assistance, taking care to avoid arousing suspicion. The refugees kept a safe distance from the Israeli agents, in case they were being watched, until they were able to meet with them. When Abba and Daniel arrived, they told the agents about everything that had happened and how they wanted to help their families and the rest of the group. They gave Abba and Daniel some money and blessed them with success.

After a month and a half, our jailers realized that we posed no threat to their cause and decided to release us. They asked us where we wanted to work, and when we told them we wanted to go back to Chomora, they took us there. This time, we were allowed to go about freely during the day, and at night, we camped out in the open without being guarded.

CHAPTER FIFTEEN

A Reunion and Escape to Sudan

Meanwhile, back in Sudan, Abba and Daniel continued making inquiries. Traveling merchants were allowed to go back and forth freely between Ethiopia and Sudan for business purposes, and Abba and Daniel asked everyone they met if they had seen us. When they reported seeing a large group of people heading toward Chomora, they immediately knew that they were talking about us.

Again, Abba and Daniel crossed the Sudan border into Ethiopia by way of the Tekezeh River, and they were detained there by soldiers who asked them if they were coming from Sudan. Abba and Daniel answered in the affirmative, adding that they had been living there for two years. "If that's the case," the soldier answered, "then welcome home!" He gave Abba a letter permitting them to go about freely in the city during the day, but at night, they had to stay in the same camp as ourselves.

Abba and Daniel knew that they couldn't live right near that refugee camp because the authorities couldn't know that they were in fact part of the group of people being detained there, so they rented an apartment nearby. They knew it was extremely dangerous to be there and that if they were caught, they would pay dearly for it. However, they kept looking until they finally found us.

Finally, after four long months apart, we were reunited with Abba. Our joy knew no bounds. But there was no time to celebrate, because we knew we had to leave Ethiopia immediately and cross the border into Sudan, where the routes to Eretz Yisrael were open. We spent another month in Chomora, so close to our destination, and yet so far. We had all managed to survive the grueling journey—our men and women, our young and old. We had made it this far, and we were almost there.

Only one of us was less than enthusiastic, there in body, but her heart elsewhere: Savta Indaya.

She had survived the harrowing journey, a miracle in itself, but not for a moment during those six months did her guilt over leaving her son behind abandon her. "Kakhsai, my son," she'd moan. "I'm not leaving without my son Kakhsai. Go on ahead, I'll wait here for Kakhsai, and we'll catch up to you along the way." These words were on her lips constantly, until her last day.

Uncle Kakhsai passed away before he was able to come to Eretz Yisrael. Until today, we don't know where he is buried. When some of our relatives returned to Ethiopia years later to search for their lost brother, they were told that he was killed in the war. That was the only piece of information we ever found out about his fate.

Savta Indaya passed away in 5741 (1981). When she died, our entire world came to a halt. Everyone was involved in the preparations for her burial. We escorted her thirty kilometers out of Chomora to the area of a local cemetery. Kayas Tefesahaku, Abba, and some other men dug a grave beneath a tall tree situated not far from the cemetery. There, near the Tekezeh River, surrounded by her loved ones, we buried Savta Indaya's body, and her *neshamah* returned to its Source.

Savta had refused to leave while her son was still in prison, and her children had taken her by force. Now, they stood beside her grave and wept, knowing they couldn't take her with them, and had no choice but to continue onward without her.

A Reunion and Escape to Sudan

Kayas Tefesahaku took a small branch from the tree and planted it near Savta Indaya's grave. He took a bit of the drinking water we had left and watered the branch in the hope that it would grow and remain there as a sign that Savta Indaya was buried there. And indeed, after we had settled in Eretz Yisrael, two of her children, Genetu and Shammai, along with Kayas Tefesahaku, returned to her burial site and found the small branch that was now fully grown. They took Savta's remains back to Eretz Yisrael, where she was reburied in Ashdod.

Our only comfort was the fact that Savta had merited a kosher burial. There were many others who died and were buried along the way without the respect due to them, but Savta Indaya was fortunate that so many people were there to mourn her passing, venerable Kayasim among them.

After the funeral, Abba laid out his plan. "We will sneak across the border, group by group," he said. The first group would consist of twenty-five boys. They arranged the day and time, and at the appointed hour, they marched through the darkness behind Abba and Daniel, all of them terrified, until they crossed the border into Sudan without incident. It had all gone smoothly, with no delays or obstacles.

As soon as they arrived, the boys went straight to the Israeli agents and registered with them. After a few days, Abba and Daniel returned to Chomora where the second group was ready and waiting to go, but the Tekezeh River had overflowed its banks and was now impassable. Abba and Daniel were petrified, fully aware that if they were caught planning escape routes, they'd suffer a bitter fate. They had no choice but to wait four months until spring, when the winter rains subsided enough for the water level to return to normal. Again, they set a day and time and forded the Tekezeh River into Sudan. From there, they proceeded to go to Gedarif and to the agents appointed by Israel. Until

5741 (1981), each group who tried to cross the border got there safely. The last group, comprised of sixty men, decided they wouldn't split up into two as they had originally planned since everything had gone smoothly until then.

When they reached the other side of the river, they were met by border guards. The soldiers surrounded the group, with Abba and Daniel at the forefront. "Who gave you permission to cross the border? Where did you come from? Who are you?" they asked. While he was trying to respond, Abba said one word for which he was rewarded by a vicious beating: "*Ma'alesh*," Abba had said. "I am sorry." He was hoping for clemency, but had only succeeded in further arousing their wrath. "Where did you learn Arabic?" the soldier bellowed, and started to thrash Abba with the pole he held in his hand. "You are smugglers! Terrorists!" he yelled accusingly.

The soldiers bound Abba's and Daniel's hands, slapped them in their faces, and threw them onto the ground, bound and beaten. They crushed Abba's right leg so badly that his knee burst from its joint. The pain was so excruciating that Abba screamed himself hoarse. Then, one of the soldiers grabbed hold of Abba's twisted leg and pulled it straight with such force that Abba cried out again in agony. Abba and Daniel were dragged away from the rest of the group, who were meanwhile taken to the refugee camp in Tenedva. We had no word from my father and Daniel for eight months, with no idea where they were or what was happening to them. We heard all sorts of rumors, but the uncertainty was worse than anything.

We found out later that Abba and Daniel had been imprisoned in Chandayit. One of the Israeli agents came to the prison and offered one of the guards a good amount of money to release them, which he did. Abba and Daniel were then taken to the refugee camp in Wadi

A Reunion and Escape to Sudan

al Chilo, among other Jews, Christians, and Muslims. They spent one night there, and the next night, they boarded a truck once again. On the way, the truck was stopped by soldiers at a checkpoint, who quickly discovered that Abba and Daniel had no travel permits to Gedarif. The soldiers debated what to do with them until Abba approached one of the soldiers and offered him money. After conferring with his comrades, he named a sum. Abba, Daniel, and the others collected the amount from among themselves, but were then left penniless. "If we give you all our money, we won't have any left for the bus," Abba said. The soldier to whom they gave the money told them that that was their problem. He then stopped a passing truck and ordered its driver to take them to Gedarif.

When Abba and Daniel arrived in Gedarif they went straight to the agents to determine our whereabouts. They were told that we were in Tenedva, an eight-hour bus ride from Gedarif, while Daniel's family was there in Gedarif.

The time had come for the two men to go their separate ways. They had been through so much together, helping each other, hurting, and rejoicing together, that it was hard for them to part. They hugged and patted each other on the back, blessing each other: "You should arrive safely, and we will meet again in Yerushalayim." Daniel joined his family in Gedarif, but Abba was afraid that since there were so many refugees in Gedarif, it would be hard to find an apartment. We settled in Tuvava, five minutes away from Gedarif. Abba rented an inexpensive apartment there while continuing to search for a place in Gedarif. As he had predicted, it was difficult to find an apartment in Gedarif, so four and sometimes more families would live together in one apartment. Tuvava was one of the four refugee camps through which Jews and non-Jews alike came through, seeking asylum from the difficult conditions in

Ethiopia. Another refugee camp, Um Rekuva, was unbearably crowded. There wasn't enough food for all the refugees, and the unsanitary conditions caused disease outbreaks and epidemics. Nearly thirteen hundred people died there within just a few months. Abba continued looking for an apartment in Gedarif, and finally, after three weeks of searching, he found something suitable and we moved in.

CHAPTER SIXTEEN

Anticipation

After surmounting all the obstacles we had encountered, we finally arrived in Sudan. We hoped that from there, our *aliyah* to Eretz Yisrael would happen immediately, just like Parda Aklum had described to us back in our village, but it didn't turn out that way. Our stay in Sudan lasted much longer than we had expected, stretching out over days, months, and even years. Our dream, which we hoped would be fulfilled quickly, now seemed once again just beyond our reach, cloaked in a fog we could not penetrate.

We spent two years in Sudan. We changed our names and tried to make ourselves as comfortable and settled as possible. The men went out to work, but the women didn't go out much. Abba worked near the apartment in Gedarif; his job was searching for water sources. There was also a well nearby, providing water for drinking and washing.

One day, while I was playing with friends near the well, I heard Savta Adiyeh calling me: "*Mitzllal, ya Mitzllal, ni'i mah.* (Mitzllal, hey Mitzllal, come here.)" I recognized her voice and ran home. I saw her standing in the courtyard outside the house, holding a small jug in her hand. "This is for you!" she said, and put it into my hand. The sight of the jug filled me with joy and excitement. Until that day I would usually stand by the side of the well and watch all the girls who came to draw water. They would lower the rope with the jug attached into the well and then pull it up, filled to the top with water. I watched and waited with anticipation for the moment when I, too, could draw water.

By giving me the jug, my grandmother gave me the message that I was now independent, free, responsible. I thanked her, gave her a hug and a kiss, and then ran to show my mother the jug. I asked her permission to draw water for Savta. My mother agreed, and then reminded me what I already knew, that I had to stand at a safe distance from the mouth of the well. I hurried back to the well, carrying the jug on my back, and even though it was the first time I did it, I felt like I had done it before and was completely familiar with the process. I slowly lowered the rope until the jug touched the water. When I felt that the jug was full, I pulled on the rope until the jug reached the mouth of the well. I was elated; I had done it!

I started walking toward Savta's house with the jug on my back. When Savta took the jug to empty it of water, there was only a little bit left. I realized that in my hurry to bring her the water, I had spilled some along the way, but it didn't take away from my happiness. I told Savta that I would bring her more water, and without waiting for a reply, I took off and ran back to the well with the jug on my back once again. I went back and forth four times. The fourth time, I tripped on a rock and fell, and the jug shattered into pieces. I felt awful, but the feeling only lasted for a moment.

The *Ribono Shel Olam* blessed me with plenty of strength and energy, and I was never bored. I always found something to do. My mother later told me that I never sat down for an instant; I was always busy. During the winter, I took it upon myself to cut trees and branches to use for cooking and heating, even though it was men's work. I joined my father and his friends and worked at full steam with no thought for the differences in age and strength between me and them. When it got

Anticipation

too quiet, someone would always ask, "Where's Mitzllal? How come we don't hear her?" because there was always something happening when I was around.

One warm day, my mother sent me to bring some water for Abba to drink while he was working. When I got there, I saw two people: one of them was pulling on a rope and bringing up sand and rocks, and the other was dumping them out someplace else. I got closer and saw Abba standing in a hole they had been digging. The hole was so deep I couldn't see the bottom of it, and I was afraid Abba would somehow fall through the bottom into the abyss. I wanted him to get out of there as quickly as possible. "Step away, it's dangerous," my father warned. He could see me from the hole. I moved away, and I saw the two men pulling on the rope that Abba was holding on to until he was out of the hole. His face was covered with dirt and dripping with sweat. I felt bad for him, seeing him like that, but I was relieved that he was out of that hole, and I hoped that he'd never go down there again.

Abba and his friends were good workers, so the bosses offered them two weeks' work outside the city harvesting wheat. Even though the work was grueling, they would be paid a decent wage, so Abba and his friends agreed. Little did they know what was awaiting them…

They traveled an entire day by truck, and when they arrived at the huge wheat field, the place was totally deserted. The foreman gave them a bag of food, explained what they had to do, and then told them that he'd be back in two weeks to get them!

Abba and his friends completed the job, and when the two weeks had gone by, they waited to be picked up. To their dismay, two weeks became two months—two months of waiting, uncertainty, and fear. The foreman eventually returned. He looked over their work, and satisfied, he paid them and brought them back to Gedarif by truck. From then on, Abba wouldn't leave Gedarif for all the money in the world, and he went back to his digging job.

One day, I ran home crying from fright. Ima rushed out at the sound of my screams, and when she saw me, she couldn't believe what her eyes were seeing. Bloody tears were pouring from both of my eyes, drying on my cheeks and my blouse, leaving huge stains in their wake. My mother also started screaming, and she was quickly joined by Savta Adiyeh. "If I hadn't seen this with my own eyes," my mother said, "I would never have believed that such a thing could happen." Then she said, "Mitzllal, my daughter, for a full year you made the impossible journey from Ethiopia to Sudan, and you never complained, never asked to ride on the donkey. You were always looking for ways to help and make things easier for others and never be a burden. Everyone talked about it, saying, 'Aseresah and Zegayu's daughter is so brave.' It could be that such talk put an *ayin hara* on you," she said.

In hindsight, I can see that those strange tears were a brief glimpse into the future, a sign that the end of our harrowing journey did not necessarily mean the end of my troubles. Even when we'd reach our long-awaited destination of Eretz Yisrael, life wasn't expected to be without obstacles, and how much more so until we actually got there and settled down.

Eventually, we forgot about the bloody tears. People started leaving one after the other, and while we were waiting our turn, my sister Esther was born, *b'siman tov u'mazel tov*. When she was nine months old, we were notified that our turn had finally arrived.

Clandestine preparations began. We sold the little that we had and started getting ready for the next phase of our trip. We were three days away from fulfilling a dream of two thousand years. *Three days.*

Anticipation

Another three days until we brought an end to our pain and suffering. Even I, so young at the time, waited with all my heart for the day I'd take my first step in the golden city of Yerushalayim.

Exactly three days before our departure, I became extremely ill and vomited uncontrollably. My parents weren't certain which took priority—their sick daughter or Eretz Yisrael and Yerushalayim. In the end, they decided not to wait. If they wouldn't go then, they told themselves, they didn't know when they'd get another opportunity to leave, if at all. They were comforted by the fact that there would be modern medical care in Eretz Yisrael. Meanwhile, my parents used the local doctor and the medication he gave me, but it didn't help. Those who made the journey with us from Ethiopia to Sudan remembered me as the brave little girl, while those who traveled with us to Eretz Yisrael remembered me as the girl who was extremely ill throughout the entire way home.

CHAPTER SEVENTEEN

On the Way: Yerushalayim Shel Zahav

A new day was breaking in the world, a day we had been anticipating for so many years. On this day, we were finally going to emerge from darkness and step into light.

An Ethiopian guide, one of the appointed agents from Gedarif, brought us and two other families to a bus idling nearby. We were parting from the past and facing the future. Thousands of years had passed while our people had waited for this dream to be fulfilled. Thousands of years of wandering, persecution, and suffering; thousands of years that the Beta Yisrael wandered from place to place. These painful years were now coming to an end. Abba took the staff he'd carried since he was a young boy tending sheep, which was passed down from generation to generation, and laid it down to rest. He boarded the bus, and instead of holding the staff in his hand as he had always done, he now carried his children, the few possessions he owned, and the excitement that the dream of Ethiopian Jewry was about to be fulfilled.

We traveled for an entire day until we arrived at the airport. For the first time in our lives, we boarded an airplane and sat on chairs. There were other travelers on board who had no connection to the clandestine operation. We, however, were still as stones. We couldn't believe that the moment we had anticipated for so long was finally coming to pass right before our eyes. On the other hand, we were terrified of disappointment: Was this really going to bring an end to our pain and isolation? Were we really going to finally merit being united with our fellow Jews? Were we really going to be free? Would we be able to finally declare, without fear, that we were Jews?

I was not yet seven years old. I had my own thoughts and feelings. I remembered the wonderful secret I'd heard, the secret of Yerushalayim Shel Zahav, and I wanted to see it with all my heart. I'd traveled an entire year on foot. I'd witnessed horrible things and had been brutally persecuted. I couldn't wait for the moment when I would actually feel my feet on the ground of my Yerushalayim.

The airplane took off and rose higher and higher into the sky while I sat in my seat, imagining my new house and my white-skinned Jewish brethren. In the middle of my reverie, I noticed a man standing at the front of the plane who had begun speaking in English. In an effort to make us understand, he held up three pictures of airplanes. He shook his head at the first two, and then nodded at the third. We understood that after the third airplane, we would be in Yerushalayim. We were still in a state of shock. Was this really it? Was this the end of that long grueling journey we had been traveling for thousands of years?

After a few hours of travel, the view changed drastically: instead of rural villages, wells, sand, mountains, camels, and donkeys, we now looked upon tall buildings and automobiles, a fast-paced world totally removed from the one we had left just a few hours earlier. The first plane landed at 3:00 p.m. in France. The passengers hurried to disembark while we sat and waited for the next phase, which came soon enough. A man and woman dressed in white robes boarded the plane and asked in Arabic, "Where is the sick little girl?" Abba, sitting by my side, was afraid to reply, but after they repeated their question again, he said to himself that he had nothing to lose by responding.

"Here she is," he said, pointing at me.

"And who is her father?" asked the woman dressed in white.

"I am!" said Abba.

"The two of you, come with us," they said, and waited for us to join them.

Abba held my hand as we disembarked, frightened but hopeful. "We'll finally get you some good medical care," he said.

As we stepped off the airplane, an ambulance that was waiting whisked us off to the hospital. When we got there, we followed our two guides into an examination room. In the meantime, my father memorized the exact route we'd taken from the ambulance to the exam room.

I lay down on the bed, and a doctor examined me, gave me shots, and instructed me to swallow some pills. Abba did not leave my side for even a moment.

Suddenly, a man in a blue uniform came into the room, walked up to Abba, and looked him in the eyes. "*We'en tisiri?*" he asked in Arabic. "Where is your passport or visa?" Abba understood the question, but since he didn't have a visa, he pretended he didn't understand what the policeman wanted. He very well remembered the last time he'd spoken Arabic and how much trouble he'd gotten into as a result.

Abba stood completely still while the policeman raised his voice, shouting, "Where is your passport?" Abba remained silent, and the policeman began searching his clothing until he found what he was looking for. He looked inside the passport and then walked out of the room toward a nearby pay phone. Suddenly, we heard him laughing hysterically, and he came back in holding Abba's passport. My father was terrified. What would happen now? How could he escape while his daughter was stuck in the hospital bed? *I have no other choice than to stay with her,* he said to himself. Then, to his great surprise, the policeman gave him back his passport, and with a huge smile on his face,

On the Way: Yerushalayim Shel Zahav

turned around and left, still laughing.

Abba had no idea what to make of the policeman's strange behavior, and until today, doesn't understand why he was laughing, but once he had his passport, he was able to breathe a sigh of relief. He went to the doctor and asked him to finish what he was doing. The doctor told him to wait patiently, but Abba was done waiting. He tried to lift me off the bed and run, but the doctor, who recognized an escape attempt when he saw one, shouted at Abba to sit down. Abba, realizing he had no other option, complied with the doctor and sat down.

When the doctor finished doing what he had to, a woman came in, and speaking in Hebrew, told us that we should follow her.

As we walked after her, Abba realized that we were not walking in the same direction from which we had come. He had memorized the entire route, and so, taking my hand, we started walking in the direction he recognized. The woman wouldn't let him go by and pointed him in the opposite direction. Abba turned around again, and again, the woman told him to go the other way. At some point, she pushed Abba and myself into a very small room and came in after us. The door closed behind her, and she pressed a button on the right side of the door. To Abba's terror, the room began rising! He had never heard of such a thing in his life. What was that wall blocking our way? Where were we going? Abba banged his hand on the door, but it wouldn't open. I held his hand as hard as I could; we were petrified. Where was this woman taking us? Did she have any connection with the laughing policeman?

As soon as Abba conceded defeat and decided to go along with the woman, the door opened, and we found ourselves outside the small room. We followed the woman outside, and the sight in front of us only increased our anxiety: there was no sign at all of the airplane. There was a bus standing at the side of the road, and she pointed at it and told Abba to board. Abba refused, looking for the airplane where his family and the others were so that he could get back onto it. *Had they left without us for Yerushalayim?* he wondered. "I want the airplane!" he shouted. "Where are you taking us? Where is my family?" The lady started pushing us toward the waiting bus, its doors open to accept us. With no choice, Abba took my hand, and we got on the bus, with the woman getting on behind us. To our surprise, all the people from the airplane were there on the bus! They had seen what was happening outside but didn't dare say a word to calm us down and let us know that they were there. The fear silenced them. They sat like statues in their places and didn't dare reply for the good or the bad.

The bus started to move while Abba told Ima everything that had happened from when we got off the plane. Ima interrupted, telling him that she had left the radio on the airplane. Abba remembered seeing one of the people with a radio like ours and asked him for it, and then he tried to explain to our guide about the forgotten radio, which was in one of the storage bins. Seeing how important the radio was to Abba, she made a quick call and got off the bus. After a few minutes, she got back on with the radio in her hand. This proved to us that she was on our side, and our anger toward her faded away.

Despite my visit to the hospital, I wasn't feeling any better; I continued throwing up during the entire time we were on the bus. After a little while, the bus stopped in front of a building with Hebrew writing on it. We got off the bus and were greeted by a crowd of people shouting instantly recognizable slogans: "Magen David! Yisrael!" they shouted, expecting us to reply enthusiastically to their greetings, but we didn't say anything. We got off the bus silently, afraid and disbelieving, afraid to celebrate or show excitement. There was a constant fear that followed us everywhere.

On the Way: Yerushalayim Shel Zahav

We entered the hotel and walked up to the reception desk, and the first thing the clerk said was, "Where is the sick girl?" Again, Abba took me to an examination room, and again I got shots and swallowed pills. After he finished, the doctor showed Abba where his room was and told Abba to wake him up if I vomited again. Abba understood and thanked him, and the doctor showed us how to get back to the lobby. We were shown to our rooms, to showers and beds, and hoped that we could shake off some of our overwhelming fatigue.

While everyone slept, my parents remained awake and at my side throughout the entire night. Every time I took even a sip of water, I threw it back up. The doctor came back in the morning and Abba reported my condition. They took me back to the examination room and gave me more shots and more pills, but they only provided temporary relief.

At 3:00 p.m., we packed up our few possessions, got back onto the bus, and soon boarded another airplane.

"Yisrael!" people called out to us. "Israel! Today!" they said. "Yerushalayim!"

We all understood what they were saying, but we were powerless to respond. I was still feeling terrible. None of the medication they'd given me had helped, but even so, I knew that today was the day we were going to Yerushalayim. Between my bouts of vomiting, I was able to look out the window, and I couldn't wait to get there. I was very curious about what awaited us and looked forward to finally being united with my Yerushalayim.

The airplane took off, and we landed a short while later. A few people disembarked while we sat in silence. Then the airplane took off again, and I turned to look out the window. The sky was totally black, but I could see far-off lights twinkling in the darkness. My heart started beating faster; I was certain without a shadow of a doubt that *this* was Yerushalayim Shel Zahav, sparkling with gold. This was the beautiful place I'd heard so much about!

Despite my still being deathly ill, I was in high spirits. The plane began to descend, and suddenly I could see out the window clearly. This wasn't really Yerushalayim Shel Zahav, I saw, and the lights I saw were regular street lights. Undaunted, I looked all around for a sign of the gold of Yerushalayim Shel Zahav, but it was nowhere to be found.

CHAPTER EIGHTEEN

Landing in Eretz Yisrael!

As the plane prepared to land, my vomiting got worse. The guides from Israel were starting to shout, "Yisrael! Yisrael! Yerushalayim!" but we were still skeptical. Even after the plane landed, not a single one of us rose from our places. We remembered the man showing us pictures of three airplanes, and we all sat and waited for the third airplane that would bring us to Yerushalayim.

"This is Yisrael!" they were saying. "Yerushalayim! Yerushalayim!" We started to exit slowly, one after the other, but we were still uncertain and frightened. Where, exactly, were we?

Then we saw an Ethiopian man approaching us. "Is this Eretz Yisrael?" Abba asked him, and he said that it was. "If so," asked Abba, "are you familiar with Geneto and Tzahayeh?"

"Yes," he replied, "and they have another brother named Shammai." These were my mother's brothers who had come to Eretz Yisrael years earlier.

"It's the truth," said Abba. "This is Eretz Yisrael!"

We had come home; our dream was finally fulfilled! For thousands of years, from generation to generation, Ethiopian Jews dreamed of arriving in the holy land. What should we do now that we finally arrived? Intuitively, everyone knelt down on their knees and kissed the ground beneath their feet. The children copied their parents and did as they did, bending their little knees and kissing the ground with their mouths. Many people had tears running down their faces. Even my little heart filled with joy and my face glowed with happiness and exaltation. The secret I'd kept in my heart now burst forth:

"Shalom, Yerushalayim, shalom,

Shalom, my dear home, shalom,

My dream has come true, and I've come home to you,

Shalom my dear home, shalom!"

We were greeted joyfully upon our arrival. Finally, we were surrounded by our Jewish brethren! The end to fear and worry had come. From now on, we would be able to serve Hashem openly. I was feeling so many things.

Amid the sounds of celebration, laughter, and tears, I suddenly heard a ringing sound that distracted me from my surroundings. The ring continued without stopping, and I found myself leaping off the sofa in the direction of the telephone. I lifted the receiver. "Shalom, Rachel," I heard the voice at the other end of the line saying. *Wait a minute,* I thought. *Who is Rachel? I am Mitzllal,* I said to myself.

"Who is this?" I asked.

"My name is Chaim, from this and this company, and I am taking a survey…"

Before he finished speaking, I answered, "I'm sorry but I can't answer you," and hung up the phone.

I returned to the couch, landing with a thump back to reality. I wasn't little Mitzllal any longer. I was seated on the couch in my own home, married with children. Years had passed since that fateful day when my feet touched the holy ground of Eretz Yisrael for the first time. So many things had happened since then, yet those feelings have remained in my heart until today. The sudden ringing of the phone had disconnected me from the wave of feelings I'd been experiencing moments before, and I suddenly felt so alone and tearful, aching with sadness, and the question returned to me with full force: *Why do I feel this way, and when and where did it begin?*

CHAPTER NINETEEN

New Name, New Beginning

I leaned back on the couch and continued my recollections. I returned to the memory of the airplane landing, the noise, and the commotion; to the joy, the prayers, and the excitement; and to the bus that brought us to the offices at the airport. I remembered the ambulance that came and took Abba and myself into the building so that I could be treated. Two people escorted us to the ambulance, one of them Ethiopian and the other Israeli.

When we got to the doctor's office, they asked Abba my name. "Mitzllal," he answered, but the Ethiopian man claimed, "I'm not familiar with this name." Apparently, he came from the Amhara region where the name Mitzllal was uncommon. The Israeli turned to him and said, "If Tzahayeh was here, he would definitely know the meaning of the name so that we could translate it into Hebrew." When Abba heard this, his eyes widened. He asked them, in broken Amharic, "Does Tzahayeh have two brothers named Geneto and Shammai?" The man replied in the affirmative, and Abba explained that his wife was the sister of Tzahayeh. The man translated Abba's words to the Israeli, who started shouting my mother's name out loud: "Zegayu! Zegayu!" He went to look for Ima, and when he found her, he introduced himself as Michah Feldman, and told her he managed the Sochnut. Together with Uncle Tzahayeh, he assisted in the *aliyah* for Ethiopian Jews. He added that Tzahayeh had worked the morning shift that day and had already gone home.

New Name, New Beginning

When Ima heard all of this, she cried from joy and grief at the same time: joy that her family was finally reunited, this time for good, and grief that the head of the family wasn't with us in the Holy Land he had dreamed of for so many years. Saba, my mother's father, had died when she was young. Savta, who had undertaken the journey to Eretz Yisrael against her will, had passed away so close to fulfilling the dream, and her brother Kakhsai had been left behind in prison.

When the doctor finished treating me, we joined the others in the office where the Sochnut agents were waiting to question and register us. When our turn arrived, our entire family stood together. They asked Abba my name once again, and he replied, "Mitzllal."

"If I were to ask you to give her a Jewish name," asked the agent, "which one would you choose?"

"Rachel," Abba replied.

My sister Alofo was soon renamed Elisheva, and Migbei was given the name Rivka. Our fellow travelers were asked the same question, and their replies were similar: Sarah, Rivka, Rachel, Leah—all names of the holy *Imahot*.

I liked the name Rachel and the feeling of renewal it represented: a new name, a new land, and a new beginning. After they finished questioning us at five in the morning, they told us that we would be going to Ohr Akiva, but we would be staying in caravans until our departure. On our way there, we saw sprinklers watering the grass, and along with everyone else, they frightened me: why was this thing running after me and trying to catch me? Our guide saw our fear and held up the sprinkler in her hand to calm us down. "It's just water," she said. She dried her hands with a smile and brought us to the caravan.

We children were very tired, so we all lay down in one bed while Ima waited for Abba to return. Sometime after sunrise, Uncle Kakhsai's daughter Tzahainesh (which means "sun") came. She had arrived in Eretz Yisrael earlier as part of a different group. When she was informed that her aunt had arrived, she took some coffee and cookies with her and went directly to our caravan. Ima hugged and kissed her niece, the daughter of her brother, whose children were all that were left to remember him by.

CHAPTER TWENTY

Identity in Question

Once we arrived in Eretz Yisrael, I was simply elated, drunk with happiness, and I walked around in a happy daze. This blissful period lasted for a mere two weeks. Just two weeks! Two weeks of learning how to bridge the gap to our new life and two weeks of pure joy, until storm clouds suddenly moved in over our lives.

We received information from our Israeli neighbors that was a complete shock. It was like we were struck by lightning out of the blue on one fine day. Throughout all the years we lived in Ethiopia, we kept the mitzvot to the best of our abilities and believed, with the purest faith, in the *Borei Olam*. Now we were informed that, according to Torah law, Ethiopian Jews were considered "*safek Yehudi*," of uncertain Jewish lineage, and therefore, required immersion in a *mikvah*, as though we were being "converted" to Judaism! "Even Kayas Yitzchak, who had escaped to Eretz Yisrael sometime in the eighties, immersed himself. "You need to be purified after all the years you lived surrounded by so many non-Jews," we were told.

This decision was a shocking assault on our heritage. We couldn't absorb the fact that our deeply-rooted Jewish identity that had been so ingrained in us throughout all the years of our exile was suddenly being called into question. Each of us responded differently to the halachic decision, but the insult it engendered was felt keenly by all of us. Those not yet married refused to immerse and threatened to leave Eretz

Yisrael rather than submit to the injustice being perpetrated against us, and indeed, many did leave. The immigrant families felt insulted and denigrated, but with humility and respect to Torah leaders, they accepted the decision to immerse themselves. They were not about to leave Eretz Yisrael after going through so much suffering to fulfill a dream that was accompanying them for so many years. This was our home, and these were our brothers. The fact that Kayas Yitzchak had immersed himself in the *mikvah* gave us the encouragement we needed to go through with it. The *kayasim* were the leaders of the community, the ones who instilled the Torah within us, and we followed their lead now just as we had in Ethiopia.

Even little Mitzllal was forced to immerse along with her elders. She found herself standing near a moveable staircase that led down into a small pool of water, surrounded by strangers who explained that she must go into the water, and then immerse herself. This was no small trauma. She couldn't understand what they wanted her to do and asked herself, "What do they want from me, and why did they tell me to remove my clothing?" Mitzllal looked at the water and was terrified to go in. What a welcome we were being given by our homeland! Mitzllal looked around again, and this time she saw her mother, who whispered in her ear, "Step in, my daughter, these are pure waters. Don't be afraid! It will be all right." She understood my fear and tried to encourage me to do what I needed to do. I climbed down the stairs into the pool and submerged my head deep into the water of the *mikvah*. I came out a new girl, so different from the one I had known.

All at once, I was transformed from a playful and perpetually energetic child, who could feel herself securely nestled beneath the protective wings of Hashem, into a shy girl who hid her gifts from others, preferring to hide herself in a corner as though she didn't exist.

Identity in Question

I was seven years old when I immersed in the *mikvah*, and it left me with a very bad feeling afterward. At the time, I didn't understand what was happening to me, but later on, I began to piece together the bits and pieces of information that came my way until I figured out what the immersion was all about. I could see that even the adults were terribly affected by their experience. Gradually, over the years, a slew of questions began to build up inside of me that gave me no rest: If I was a "questionable" Jew, then who could be considered a true Jew? If my identity as a Jew was uncertain, then where did I belong? Where could I go to feel accepted if I didn't feel I belonged in Ethiopia, the land of my birth, nor in Eretz Yisrael, the Land of Our Fathers? Where could I go and feel warmth and love? Where could I feel safe and secure? How could I figure out where I belonged? Which other land could I call my home if not Eretz Yisrael?

I finally discovered the answers to these questions that had followed me for most of my life at age twenty-three, after strengthening my relationship with Hashem. When I was a child, I felt as though my world had fallen in on me, and I carried this feeling with me all throughout my childhood, my teen years, and my early adulthood.

CHAPTER TWENTY-ONE

The Absorption Center

After a short stay in the Ohr Akiva Absorption Center, we moved to Kiryat Gat.

We lived in small attached houses that stood in a long row. There was a small parcel of grass in front of each house. We hung the laundry behind the house, and we occasionally hid out there when we were playing hide-and-seek. There was a playground behind the houses across the street where we loved to play.

Because we were a family of seven, we were given two houses. Each house consisted of two rooms—a living room and a small kitchen, as well as a bathroom and shower. We used the second house primarily for storage, and we also kept the ice cream Abba brought home from his job in that house. Abba worked for the Tena Noga dairy producer from the time when we arrived in Eretz Yisrael until they closed the factory many years later, and he would bring home ice cream for all of us.

Our assigned guidance counselor was lovely. Despite the wide gaps between us and the longtime residents of Eretz Yisrael, our adjustment was relatively easy. My parents went to *ulpan* to learn Hebrew along with the rest of the adults. We were also offered all sorts of activities to help us acclimate to Eretz Yisrael. I loved the singing group most of all. My wounded soul relished the music. For Chanukah we performed in front of all the mothers and girls, and I stood before them and sang, "*Ner li ner, ner li dakik...* I have a candle, a lovely little candle..." My

The Absorption Center

mother watched me with a smile on her face. I loved to learn, I enjoyed the new beginning, and I started off on the right foot.

There was a huge lot behind a gate near the entrance to Kiryat Gat where the staff members parked their cars. Children would often play or ride bicycles there. Once, when I was playing with my friends at a playground nearby, our curiosity was aroused by the sound of music playing. We followed the sound and realized that the music was coming from a truck that was parked in the lot. All the children ran over to the driver and asked him about the music. He explained that he sold ice cream from his truck, and we learned to recognize his arrival by the sound of the music. We would then run back home and ask for money to buy ice cream.

Another time, I encountered a car that was belching thick white smoke into the street. When I saw it, I ran outside and directly into the white smoke. It was only afterward that I discovered it was an exterminator truck, and I had to stay as far away from it as possible.

On the border of that lot, there was a two-way street with tall buildings on the other side of it. We had to cross the street and walk alongside the buildings in order to get to the grocery store or to school. It was an easy route, and I walked it every day with my sisters and friends.

Two months after our arrival, elections were held in that same lot for the position of prime minister. Campaign stations lined the street, distributing brochures amid blaring music. I thought it was a holiday. My parents went to vote, and volunteers showed my parents what to do. Abba and Ima voted for Yitzchak Shamir as a show of gratitude to the Conservative faction because "they exerted themselves and did so much to help us that we voted for them, in the hope that they would continue acting on our behalf," they explained. The day after the elections, the lot was deserted, with no sign of the previous day's tumult.

I had an interesting dream around that time. In my dream, I was standing across the gate to the Absorption Center, playing with a friend on the lawn near the administration offices. Suddenly, I stopped and lifted my head skyward. I saw a colorful array of lights spilling from the sky in a rainbow arc until they hit the ground near my feet. I stood there, exhilarated by the display, and I turned to my friend in excitement. "Look at these beautiful colors!" I exclaimed. The next morning, I awoke with a smile on my face, remembering my dream. Many changes, positive changes, awaited me in my life: learning, growing, and so much joy.

CHAPTER TWENTY-TWO

Beneath the Shadow of Doubt

Throughout this period of adjustment, I was still troubled by the issue of my identity. Deep inside, I kept telling myself, "Hashem knows who is a Jew!" I decided there was one thing that I would never allow anyone to cast into doubt: my belief in Hashem, and the knowledge that I was a *bat Yisrael*, a Jewish daughter. This was the one thing about which there was no doubt, and I would never let anyone take it away from me. I buried this truth in my heart where no one would see or hear it. I knew that if my Jewish identity was taken away from me, I'd be stripped completely bare, with no remnant of myself left behind. My deep belief in Hashem was the foundation I rested upon, and it rescued and protected me all the time. "I am a Jew, without any doubt!" I would tell myself. "I know this for sure. My true self is embedded in my pure *neshamah*, and this will not be taken from me."

Time passed, but the question of my identity continued to weigh heavily upon me. The problem didn't end with the immersion I had undergone, but rather had begun with it. The doubt remained with me all the time, and I grew up beneath its shadow.

At first, I attended an *ulpan* to learn Hebrew. We were a mixed group of boys and girls of all ages. Some of the students, like myself, sat quietly and listened, while others horsed around and were even punished for their misbehavior. After a few months, we were integrated into classrooms with other Israeli children. I had always been inquisitive, and I wanted to learn. When I was in Sudan, I would see children getting onto a bus with notebooks and school bags, and I understood that they were going to school to learn. My mother couldn't believe that I remembered this, but the sight was engraved in my mind because I was so jealous of them. I also wanted to learn, and now I finally had the chance to do so.

When I started first grade, the teacher stood behind me with her hand resting on my shoulder as she introduced me to the class. I was so happy. I loved to listen and learn. Sometimes I would participate, and sometimes I would sit quietly, but I was always well behaved and a model student.

In seventh grade, I was chosen along with a group of other gifted children to take an advanced course at Machon Weitzman in Rechovot once a week, but it made me uncomfortable. I panicked when I realized that my talents had been noticed. *You must not stand out,* I told myself. Left with no choice, no desire, and no joy, I joined the group and traveled to Rechovot, but I made no effort to excel so that I wouldn't stand out. I had convinced myself that it was forbidden to excel!

In ninth grade, I was again chosen to take a course to become a youth counselor. Again, it caused me much discomfort. I had no desire to learn and grow as much as I could. *Why am I so afraid to stand out?* I asked myself. *Why am I so afraid to reach my potential, to prove myself? Where does this fear come from?*

My identity crisis continued to disturb me. Was I Mitzllal, who had no doubt at all about her Jewish identity, or was I Rachel, lost among the Jews of Israel, wondering if she were Jewish at all?

Today, I know that my parents and forefathers lived in Ethiopia and guarded their Judaism amid life-threatening danger with unfathomable strength and courage, and not once did they falter in their faith. Study houses were destroyed, there were no *sefarim*, the missionaries grew more powerful, and yet the only thing the Jews of Ethiopia sought was Jewish spiritual guidance. It was only when conditions became unbearable that it was decided to leave Ethiopia. They preferred to die trying to leave rather than knowing that they had not at least tried to get away. Guarding their identity and their G-dly image was more precious than anything. They endangered their lives to uphold their Jewish identity, and many people perished along the way.

Savta Indaya had always told us, "My children, I am already old and infirm, and I am hindering you from returning home. Leave me behind so that at least you will get there." Her words were prophetic. Amid great pain and suffering over leaving her son behind, she asked of the *Ribono Shel Olam*, "Abba, have mercy on my children that they should merit to return home. Take me to You, because I am no help to them. Please, watch over my children and let them return home." And now, after her children had finally returned home, their Judaism was suspect. Was there any fate more bitter than this?

In the land of my birth, our identity was clear both to us and to those around us. "Your home is Yerushalayim," the non-Jews would say to us, and we knew this without a shadow of a doubt. The suspicion of people regarding our identity only arose in the Land of Our Fathers.

Many years later, I asked my father, "How did you feel when you were told your Judaism was in doubt and that you had to immerse in a *mikvah*?" Abba didn't answer right away, but then he said, "I was terribly upset. They treated me like I was a *goy*! Non-Jews seeking to convert need to immerse and purify themselves, not me. Did I worship idols as a non-Jew that they should do this to me?"

We were wounded to our core. We had been welcomed to our holy homeland in the manner described in the verse, "*Muzar hayiti l'echai, v'nachri l'bnei imi*—I was a stranger to my brothers and foreign to my mother's children." Our own brothers were suspicious of us; we were strangers in their eyes! We carried this painful reality around with us, but still tried to move forward and establish ourselves in Eretz Yisrael with our developing knowledge.

I probably could have weathered this period of adjustment more easily and pleasantly if it hadn't been for this shadow of doubt that had been cast upon us. It made everything around me seem suspicious and threatening. I took every opportunity to catch the Israelis at their mistake and prove to them, or more accurately, to myself, that the doubt was coming from them and not from me. These encounters were very unpleasant. The shy and retiring Rachel would suddenly explode and lash out aggressively. Today, I understand that these outbursts were actually the voice of Mitzllal, the little girl that came to remind Rachel that she was still sheltered beneath the wings of the *Shechinah*. Mitzllal was trying to remind Rachel that she had the strength to forge ahead despite her difficulties and continue living her life.

Spiritually, I felt paralyzed. I grew up in tremendous pain, afraid to stand out, afraid to excel, afraid to add more pain to the ache I already carried around within me, every minute of the day.

CHAPTER TWENTY-THREE

A Guest in This World

Along with this pain came another. When I was seventeen, Savta Adiyeh, my father's mother, passed away. Unlike Savta Indaya, my maternal grandmother with whom I spent little time, I had tried to spend as much time as I could with Savta Adiyeh. I always enjoyed listening to adults and gathering all kinds of interesting bits of information from them, and I learned a lot from Savta's stories. During one of our visits, sitting across from her as I fed her, I could see that Savta wasn't feeling well.

Several months later, I was called to the office at school, where I was told to return home right away. I rode the bus filled with trepidation, and when I got near Savta's house, I saw a green sheet spread over the fence, a typical sign that a gathering was being prepared. The crying voices, audible from a distance, left no room for doubt: Savta Adiyeh was gone!

My whole body began to tremble. It took me a long time to recover and digest the fact that Savta was no longer alive. From our kitchen window, I could see the porch of her house where my Aunt Amuyeh would hang up the laundry. I would never see Savta's clothes hanging on the line again, and this bitter realization was painfully hard to bear.

I returned to school after the *shivah*. I tried to return to my normal routine, but found myself unable to. Savta's passing made a tremendous impression on me. I learned a lot about life from Savta's death. I poured my heart out into my diary and titled my entry, "The Guest."

When all is said and done, I wrote, *I am just a guest in this world, and my* avodah *is to become the best guest I could possibly be.* A guest goes through a lot in his life. He traipses through deserts, crosses lakes and rivers, and weathers many stormy days and nights. He wanders from place to place looking for a good place to land where he can relax and rest from his long and painful journey. I saw myself as a guest in this world; I'd been through a lot in my life, and I wanted to rest. I wanted to find my place in this great big world. In her death, Savta gave me my life, reminding me of the real truth: we are all guests here, each one with his or her own predetermined time.

The realization that I was only a guest in this world helped me arrive at the conclusion that I wanted to change. I didn't want to go on living in such pain. I understood that all I had to do was be the best possible guest. I was a guest in the house of the King Who had created this beautiful world for me and brought me into His home. Would I be the kind of guest who is grateful to the host, thanking him and blessing him for the water he gives his guest to drink, the bread he gives his guest to eat, and the clothing he gives his guest to wear? Would I merit to thank Hashem for everything He has given me, or will I be the type of guest who complains to the host all the time about why he was greeted with bread and water instead of meat, wine, and fish?

Until then, I'd been a disgruntled guest, demanding to know why my brothers had greeted me, their sister, with such suspicion. And why did Hashem doubt me? Wasn't I His daughter? But I didn't want to be an ungrateful guest! I wanted to be a guest who praises and thanks his host.

"Hashem, my Host," I said, "I want to thank You for the life and all the good You have given me. I want to learn from Your ways, Hashem, my Host, and place good deeds before You and to host You in the same beautiful and respectful way that You host me, and I want that You should receive my offerings favorably."

I gained many important insights in the wake of Savta's passing, but I still had a long way to go toward accepting myself completely.

When I was eighteen, I received a *Teudat Zehut*, an Israeli identity card. My name appeared on my parents' cards as "Mitzllal Rachel," but I didn't want that name on my card. Along with my sister Migbei, now Rivka, I went to a lawyer to request the removal of the name "Mitzllal" so that only "Rachel" would appear on the card. I also requested that my birthdate be listed, because only the year of my birth was listed on my parents' forms. These changes were made, and I was filled with relief. I had parted from my Ethiopian name and all it represented, and I looked forward to embarking on a new and unencumbered path.

I finished twelfth grade successfully. My friends wrote me words of farewell, each with a similar message: "You should reach your goals without too much effort." Now I realize that at that time, I was apathetic toward my success. I didn't invest any effort in learning and didn't even try to fulfill my potential. Today, I know that my pain stymied me and prevented me from harvesting much riper fruit.

CHAPTER TWENTY-FOUR

Stormy Resistance

Thirteen years had passed since our arrival in Eretz Yisrael. At that point, when I was twenty, I started working in the surgery ward of a Jerusalem hospital, seeking to acquaint myself with the medical field. On the one hand, I was searching for the medicine that would heal my own pain, and on the other hand, I wanted to help others in their suffering. I imagined myself as a nurse who could help others, be a real sister in their pain, and listen, understand, identify, and offer encouragement and support.

Many of the patients in the Orthopedic Department were broken in body; some could only walk with the help of crutches, some required a wheelchair, and some were even more limited and needed help in every area. I helped them all with joy and love.

One of the patients there was an elderly woman who required assistance for everything. She needed someone to feed her, and there was no one available on a regular basis. When I saw a busy nurse heading toward her room, I offered to take over for her. She thanked me warmly and returned to her tasks. I sat across from the woman and began to patiently feed her at her own pace. As we warmed up to each other, we began to talk, and soon the woman was sharing her life story with me. After that day, the woman insisted that I be the only one to feed her, and I agreed.

I gained tremendous satisfaction from my work. There were patients

Stormy Resistance

who required physical help and those who needed a shoulder to cry on. I knew about pain, and if there was anything I could do to ease another's sorrow, I was happy to do it.

In 1996 a heated controversy arose concerning our Ethiopian community. It was during a period of frequent terror attacks, and there was a critical blood shortage. We went to donate blood along with everyone else, only to learn, to our dismay, that our blood was being discarded without even being tested. It was as if they were telling us, "Your time and effort are worth nothing to us."

A storm of protest rose up among us; if they had a doubt that our blood was tainted by disease, then why couldn't they tell us so beforehand? Why did we have to come for nothing if they weren't going to use our blood anyway?

I was devastated. I felt that my blood and the blood of my brothers were crying out from the ground. All we wanted was to be a part of the Jewish people. We admired their knowledge and wisdom, and we were hoping they would be able to teach us what they knew. We wanted to narrow the gap that fell between us to make up for all the years we were isolated in Ethiopia. We gave our blood willingly, aware that it was a matter of life and death, and after all our efforts, we discovered that they didn't want our help. This rejection was very painful. We had already been here for a number of years and felt that we were already beyond such issues, but the rejection of our blood revived all the negativity we initially felt. We were still being viewed as "*safek*" Jews, "*safek*" disease carriers. Would we ever escape from this shadow?

In response, the Ethiopian community organized a large demonstration in front of the Health Ministry. Knesset member Ediso Masala stood up and shouted, "Our blood is not black, it is RED!" Everyone present could identify with that, and we shouted out in pain. The

Minister of Health also stood up to speak. I don't remember exactly what he said, and in any case, what could he have possibly said? How could his words mollify us? The demonstration soon turned violent, and people started throwing rocks in anger. Mounted police armed with guns and clubs had been circulating during the demonstration, covered from head to toe with protective gear, but whom were they protecting themselves against? Unarmed men, women, and children who had come to express their pain and frustration. Some of the youths began to throw rocks at the police, and then ran off to hide from the tear gas that had been used in response.

On our way home from the demonstration, we were approached by an English-speaking reporter who asked us, "Tell me how you feel today after all that has happened?"

His question hit me like a bomb. This was the first time anyone had asked me how I felt. I had waited so long for this question! Until then, I had always been listening to others speak, sharing their sorrows and offering advice, but not once had anyone asked me about how I felt! No one had ever asked me how I felt about the theft of my identity, how devastated I was when I was told my Judaism was suspect, and how I dealt with it for so many years. No one had ever considered the impact the forced immersion in the *mikvah* had made on my life. I was so little, and the immersion had been a traumatic turning point for me. I was never the same again after that. That one event had stirred up pain in me that followed me wherever I went and gave me no rest. In any case, nobody had ever bothered to find out what had caused such a drastic change in my personality, and nobody had ever tried to heal my wounds.

At first, I stood speechless in front of the reporter, and with all these thoughts running through my head, I didn't know what to say. I didn't know if the reporter was a Jew. If he was, then perhaps he would understand the damage that had been done to me and my identity. If he wasn't Jewish, there was no way he would understand.

Until today, I am grateful to that reporter and his question. It was a breath of fresh air and created a small opening in my closed and wounded heart. I had been longing for someone to ask me how I felt and to offer some help. I had been searching for so long for a spiritual guide, someone who would remove the doubt that had been placed upon me and my identity, someone who would open doors for me, take an interest in me, and accompany me in my new life. I searched, but had not yet found anyone willing to rise to the task.

Now, in front of a camera and microphone, someone was finally asking me to express my feelings. For the first time in my life, I was able to respond, melding together the thoughts in my mind and the feelings in my heart. Overwhelmed, I began to cry, my tears dating back to the start of my journey from Ethiopia, but my mind was clear and sharp. Then I regained my power of speech.

"I am disappointed," I declared. "Very disappointed with the way we have been treated here. My ancestors suffered terribly in Ethiopia because of their Judaism, and we went through fire and water to get here, and yet all these difficulties were nothing compared to the pain of rejection we are feeling in our own homeland. Every one of these protestors sacrificed everything to merit coming to Eretz Yisrael, and now their dreams have been shattered right before their eyes." I finished speaking, dried my tears, and continued walking onward with my friends, lost in thought.

The reporter trailed after us, wanting to ask more questions, but I couldn't talk anymore. I asked myself if it would have been better if I had remained in Ethiopia, where I had lived without any doubts at all, fighting for my Judaism against the non-Jews rather than with my own people?

I returned to the demonstration in my mind's eye. I saw my brother Nogosa bending down to pick up a rock near his feet, then throwing it at one of the mounted police. The rock hit the officer's foot, and he turned his horse around in the direction the rock had come from, brandishing a club in his hand. Nogosa ran off and was swallowed up by the crowd and my cries, "Run, Nogosa! Run!" fell on deaf ears.

I turned in another direction and I saw a man of about sixty or seventy standing on a hilltop. He was trying with all his might to throw a stone, but it kept landing at his feet. Behind him were some boys throwing rocks and hitting the police. One of the policemen saw them and fired tear gas at them, and they ran up the hill and hid themselves from the assault. The old man turned around and tried to climb up the rock and hide as well, but he slipped, rolled backward, and fell. Eventually he stood up, took hold of the boulder, and climbed up the hill after them. At the top, he adjusted his *ne'atzelah*, a wide white scarf worn around the shoulders. Tears rolled down his face and his lips were moving. I was too far away to hear what he was saying, though I wanted very much to know.

This image hurt even more than the one of the policeman chasing my brother. I didn't know the man, but I could identify with his pain. "You made this horrific journey," I said to myself. "Your heart was filled with expectations, and when things didn't go as planned, you were disappointed." I realized we were both afraid, he for the future of our children, and myself for how my life would be once I, *b'ezrat Hashem*, reached his age. Would the future be different, and better, than the past?

Stormy Resistance

The pain was shared by all of us. We were pushed away by the non-Jews of Ethiopia where we fought tooth and nail, with no weapons at our disposal, to guard our Judaism, and now we were being rejected in the Land of Our Fathers and fighting with our own people!

The demonstration reminded me of a fight that had broken out while we were still in the Absorption Center in Kiryat Gat shortly after our arrival. There was a rumor that a man had been passing the buildings across from the center on his way to the grocery store when someone dumped a carton of cottage cheese on him. He didn't see who threw it, but he could tell from which direction it had come. After a few days, we heard another story of the same thing happening to someone else in the same spot. Someone else was pelted with eggs, and even though he tried to clean himself off, the smell proved the truth of his story. Another man, at the same place, was hit by a stone.

One day, I was walking to school by myself along the path between the buildings. For some reason, my sisters, Alofo and Migbei, who normally accompanied me, were not there, and I didn't meet any friends along the way. Suddenly, I saw a stone rolling in my direction. I looked around but didn't see anyone. I continued walking, and from the corner of my eye, I saw a man hiding behind a building. I stood still so I could catch him red-handed, but he didn't dare try again, and I felt empowered. Even so, I never walked that way again. From then on, I took a different path, longer but safer.

In spite of these incidents, others continued to walk past the buildings to get to the store, and they would occasionally return with "souvenirs" on their clothing…

A while later, I saw a group of men and boys from the Absorption Center gathered on the road outside the gate, throwing rocks at the people on the other side in response to the attacks being made against them. They were blocking traffic so the police were called, as well as ambulances to carry away the wounded victims of the buildings across the way.

It took this show of force for our "neighbors" to realize that their attacks would not be tolerated and they would have to adjust to the newcomers across the road at the Absorption Center.

When I asked my parents what caused this protest to break out, they explained that we had done nothing to bring on these attacks. They simply didn't like the fact that we were there and that we looked so different. I thought about this every time I heard the words "*kushi*" and "*kushit*" (literally, "black," but used pejoratively to describe Ethiopian Jews). When I was young and starting to understand the meaning of the term, I realized this was an insult used to describe black-skinned non-Jews. I didn't understand the connection between us and them, because I was a Jew. Even though my skin was black like theirs, we were completely different! My heart pinched at the comparison. Not only was I not considered a Jew, now I was a "*kushit*." It was as though they were saying that the only part of us they acknowledged as certain was that we were "*kushi*." Every time I heard the word, I pretended I didn't, but my mood would change from one extreme to the other. If I had been laughing, my smile would disappear. If I'd be talking to my friends, I would immediately shut down. A wall of silence would rise up around me.

CHAPTER TWENTY-FIVE

Caution: Missionaries!

After working for a year in the hospital, I realized that I didn't want to continue pursuing the medical field. I had devoted a full year to helping others cope with their pain, but where would my healing come from? I realized that the medicine I was seeking could only come from within me. The time had come to help myself, without anyone else's assistance.

When I was twenty-one, I went to study marketing and management at one of the colleges in Jerusalem, but I could not connect with this course of study. I was emotionally paralyzed, in pain and introverted. My pain was hindering me from functioning normally in my life. Ever since my childhood, this pain had prevented me from being a normal girl who ran around and played like little Mitzllal. Rachel, as opposed to Mitzllal, would analyze every single thing she did, worrying about what other people would think and say. I decided to "market" my pain to the outside world.

The foundation for every marketing plan begins with the "Four Ps": product, price, place, and promotion.

My product was my Jewish identity, and I had paid a significant price for it with constant suffering. The place of this product was here in Eretz Yisrael, in Yerushalayim, the land I'd dreamed about and longed for. I was certain this was the correct placement for my product even if others didn't agree with me. I had gone from being a recognized Jew to being an unacknowledged stranger, but I myself was never in doubt. I knew full well I was a Jew! I repeated this to myself every single day, and I felt a strong desire to publicize it via every media outlet possible.

In the course of my studies, I learned a lot about myself. I realized that I had to take control of my life, publicize my definitive product, and rid myself of the doubt that was controlling me and eating me up inside, ruining every move I made.

One day after class, I went with a friend to the Kotel. It was extremely crowded that day, filled with tourists and Jews of every stripe. Soldiers were sitting up high on the surrounding buildings, and the plaza was surrounded by policemen.

We went down the ramp that led to the women's section and looked for a place close to the lone remainder of the Beit Hamikdash. We started to pray, each of us with our own requests. It was a special prayer in a special place. I felt that Someone was listening to me, and He was so close! I knew that all prayers are answered—some of them immediately, some after a few days, and some a few months or years later. Hashem was always listening to me, and I had always found comfort for my wounds from Him.

"Abba!" I cried, "I am Your daughter, my beloved Abba, and I am a Jew! A daughter of the King! May it be Your will, *Ribono Shel Olam*, that I should merit to be a kosher Jew in my thoughts, my words, and my deeds without a shadow of a doubt, at all times, all places, and wherever I find myself!"

My Creator was the only One I could rely on; He surrounded me with His understanding and was always listening. I knew that He would accept my prayers at the right time.

After I finished praying and started to back away from the Kotel, I was suddenly aware of its stones. I saw the greenery growing out from

Caution: Missionaries!

between the stones, the doves resting on top of the stones, and all the notes folded and pressed between the cracks. Some of them had fallen onto the ground, forming little piles at the bottom of the Kotel. I saw many different types of women, and I saw the ancient stones lined along the bottom as well as the newer ones added on the top. I focused on the lower stones, and I saw in them both purity and truth. They were the remains of Hashem's House. I held them in my gaze. These were the indisputable stones of the Holy Temple, while the ones on top were extra.

Gazing at the stones, I came to the conclusion that I had to hold fast to the indisputable part of me, to my pure and honest Judaism, which was the foundation of my identity. Only then could I move forward and grow.

I looked at the stones one last time before I turned around and started walking forward. I ran my eyes from the bottom to the top, and then I lifted my head higher and thanked Hashem for listening to me, for His help and support, for helping me find the right perspective, and for the insights I'd gained.

But my journey toward my true identity was not over. I knew it was impossible to wipe away the pain of years in one day, but at least now I felt I was moving in the right direction. I'd move forward one step at a time, until the pain was behind me.

My friend and I decided to walk back to hold on to the inspiration we were feeling. We walked from the Kotel to Talpiot, quite a long way, but what was this walk to me compared to the year I'd spent walking to Sudan? Since I was a small girl, I was used to walking without complaint. We walked through the narrow and winding paths of the Old City until we came to the main road. Along the way, we'd passed the building that housed Arachim. We were reminded of the day we spent there listening to fascinating lectures and imbibing the pleasant atmosphere. We smiled when we thought about it and continued walking.

From a distance, we could see a woman, her head covered and wearing long sleeves and a skirt, looking around in all directions as though she were searching for something.

As we passed her, she turned to us and asked, "Would you like to read something interesting?" She then handed us a small book that looked like a *Chumash*. I thought at first that she was a member of Arachim, so I took the book and started to read. The words looked familiar, but then my eyes fell on something that I'd never seen in any *Chumash*. My mouth opened in shock. I started trembling, and I felt chills run through me. This woman was a *missionary*, dressed to catch people in her trap.

Even though we were terrified, we returned the book to her and started to shout, "This is *sheker*! It's all lies! It's supposed to say the name of Moshe Rabbeinu here, that the Torah was given to him by *Hakadosh Baruch Hu*, Who spoke to him, and not to the name you have written here! You're a liar!" I felt like I was waging war for my *emunah*, for my Father above.

"Beware of missionaries, Rachel. Beware of missionaries!" my Jewish soul cried out inside of me. We wanted to warn other people passing to look out for the dangerous trap hidden inside this woman, so we shouted, "Watch out for her! She's a missionary!" And we got away from her as soon as we could.

Just minutes after such an inspiring experience at the Kotel, I was being tested, as if to destroy the wonderful feeling I'd had there, but I was happy I'd been able to avoid the trap and had the courage to cry out in Hashem's Name. I was so grateful to have withstood the test.

CHAPTER TWENTY-SIX

A Trip to America

The school year had come to an end. It had been a very busy year, and I felt like I needed a break. I was desperate to shake off some of the pain I was feeling. My friend asked me to join her on a trip to America, and I agreed. Armed with our passports, visas, and suitcases, we made our way to the airport. From there, we'd fly to Canada, and then on to America.

I felt like I had left my pain behind. I traveled for a month and saw some amazing sights, breathtaking views, and many different types of people. Whenever we needed advice about kosher restaurants or a place to stay, we didn't hesitate to ask anyone wearing a *kippah*. Many of them asked us where we were from and how we knew Hebrew.

Most of the time, people were happy to help us, but there were a few who pretended they didn't hear us and kept walking. The first time it happened in New York, I naively thought that the woman didn't hear my question, so I repeated myself, this time louder. To my surprise, the woman ignored me and hurried past us. My friend laughed about it, but I was very hurt. I realized she thought I was a "*kushit*," like all the other black people in America. I remembered the slur that had stuck to me in Eretz Yisrael, and the well of sadness I'd tried to leave behind rose up in me once again.

From then on I started paying close attention to the dark-skinned people they called "*kushim*." I saw that there were variations in color, in addition to other differences among them. I tried to find the common denominator between us, but the only thing we had in common was the color of our skin. That was where our similarity ended. I had a Jewish *neshamah* that craved closeness to the One Above.

Most of the people I met on my trip were very nice, happy to help, and even happier when they discovered that I spoke Hebrew and came from Eretz Yisrael, a place they'd only dreamed about. I was warmed by the connection I felt with them and appreciated that they weren't judging me. When that would happen, my pain would recede for a while.

I saw such beautiful sights in America, and I couldn't help repeating, "How wondrous are Your works, Hashem!" over and over again. I felt so close to Hashem. I knew that there were also beautiful sights and kind people in Eretz Yisrael, and that if I would open my eyes, I would see them and soothe my pain, but I knew that this was easier said than done.

Despite the good feelings I had while traveling, I knew that my place was in Eretz Yisrael and that I would not trade it in for anywhere else. On the other hand, I was afraid to return to my struggle.

When it came time to return, I boarded the airplane and returned home into the arms of my family. They immediately noticed the change in me. "You're glowing," they said. "America was good for you! Tell us your secret!" I also felt a slight difference in myself, but I didn't want to speak of the secret pain I had been carrying around inside of me for years. That would remain hidden.

My family members were the only ones I could lean on—they felt solid and secure to me. I often confided in my mother about certain things, and she would give me wise advice in response. The pain of our rejection was the only thing I didn't speak to her about. Ima had no idea where her lively Mitzllal had disappeared to, and how Rachel had taken her place. My parents and siblings didn't really think about their status in Eretz Yisrael like I did. Only today does my mother understand what her daughter was going through during those long, hard years.

CHAPTER TWENTY-SEVEN

The Arab Messenger

Sixteen years had passed since the transformation of Mitzllal. The pain that was always with me had left me largely apathetic, but whenever Hashem sensed a small opening within me, He would send a messenger to help me on my way.

I was working as a cashier in Jerusalem Cafe. It was very crowded one morning, and when things finally calmed down at around ten thirty, I decided to take a fifteen-minute break.

I went over to speak with my friend Tami, who had become a *ba'alat teshuvah* a few months earlier. She would often share with me some of her newfound knowledge. I had always been drawn to *divrei Torah*, deriving great warmth and comfort from them. Now Tami opened a siddur and drew my attention to the introductory paragraph that is said before Grace After Meals:

A song of Ascents. When Hashem will return the captivity of Zion, we will be like dreamers. Then our mouth will be filled with laughter and our tongue with glad song. Then they will declare among the nations, "Hashem has done greatly with these." Hashem has done greatly with us, we were gladdened. O Hashem—return our captivity like springs in the desert. Those who tearfully sow will reap in glad song. He who bears the measure of seeds walks along weeping, but will return in exultation, a bearer of his sheaves. (Translation from *The Artscroll Tehillim*.)

Tami explained enthusiastically, "You see, Rachel, we're in exile now, in the desert, sowing in tears and praying for growth, but the days will come when Hashem will return His children to Zion, to Jerusalem, and it will be so wonderful, and our lives now will seem like a dream! Our mouths will be filled with laughter and true joy, and we will sing praises to Hashem. It will be a special day; everyone will stop what they are doing and watch the great kindness Hashem will do for His children. The dry desert will bloom, and we will harvest in joy and carry the sheaves on our shoulders. That day is coming!"

I felt that these words were meant for me directly. An image of our arrival from Ethiopia to Eretz Yisrael rose before my eyes. For years, returning to Eretz Yisrael was little more than a dream, and now that dream had come true. When we got here, my heart had been filled with joy, but according to Tami, it was just a small taste of the true and complete *simchah* that was yet to come.

Today, I know that the Jerusalem I had encountered as a young child was not the Jerusalem I had been dreaming of, but rather, it was completely different from what I had imagined. I was hoping to find a Jerusalem where none of its inhabitants would state, "*Tzar li hamakom hazeh*—There is not enough space here for my brothers." Now I understood why I had been so disappointed.

"You are still destroyed, Jerusalem," I whispered. "You are nowhere near the glory that will yet come to be. I had expected to see you with all your children gathered together, and I thought you'd be glowing with light, like a mother with all of her children surrounding her. Instead, my Jerusalem, I saw that you were like a woman whose children have been taken from her.

"Don't worry, Jerusalem! You are not barren! Your scattered flock will soon return to you; your glory will bring them back, and they will see you rebuilt. The house of the King will arise, and unlike the two

Holy Temples that came before, this one will stand forever. And Abba, my Father in Heaven, the great Shepherd, will rule over us and the entire world, forever. Today, for the first time, I have cried for you, Jerusalem. I know you were once beautiful, and I cry over your destruction."

As I thought deeply about what I'd learned, I understood that the unity I had been looking for in Eretz Yisrael did not yet exist. The suspicion that hung over me made me feel like I wasn't part of my people, but I soon realized that even they were not united among each other. Now, after listening to Tami, I realized that the time had not yet come for true unity, but that time would certainly come.

I felt that these verses had been composed especially for me, in order to explain to me what I hadn't been able to comprehend and to spread warmth in my wounded heart. Then Tami turned my attention to something else.

"Rachel," she said, pointing at a woman sitting nearby, reading a small pamphlet. "Do you see that woman sitting over there? She is an Arab, and she wants to convert to Judaism! She's been working at it for a few months now."

"Whaaat?" I cried out in surprise. I couldn't believe my ears. An Arab woman wanting to convert? I was shocked to the core of my being, and I couldn't hold myself back from approaching her and asking her a burning question. Tami was embarrassed and tried to stop me, but there was nothing she could do. I was determined to get the answer to my question right then and there.

When the woman saw me coming, she lifted her eyes from the page and looked at me, waiting to hear what I had to say. I asked her, "Tell me, how did you come to the decision to convert? Why did you decide to become a Jew?" The woman didn't flinch at my chutzpah; she just answered me clearly, "There is one G-d, and He is the G-d of the Jews."

Her response shocked me. I sat down again across from Tami. I saw my whole life before my eyes, running at a dizzying pace, and afterward, I grew calm. From the calm after the storm, I found the cause of my sorrow, and I realized my life would never be the same again. The woman's simple declaration kept repeating itself in my mind: *There is one G-d, and He is the G-d of the Jews.*

I suddenly remembered a promise I'd made to myself sixteen years earlier, when I had immersed in the *mikvah* and emerged so hurt and disappointed. *It makes no difference what anyone else thinks of me,* I thought to myself, *but there is one thing that nobody can doubt about me and will never be stripped from me, and that is my faith in Hashem. He will always be my Father, and I will always be His daughter.*

This one thing, my rock-solid faith in G-d, was tucked inside of me, invisible to everyone, and I never let it out. The exhilaration I felt now lifted me out of my sorrow and shined light into my life. I looked again at the Arab woman, absorbed in her learning, and I said to myself, "She is an Arab woman and she is unafraid to come close to Hashem, and I, a Jewish woman, am afraid?! How can that be possible? If I know what the right thing to do is, how can it be that I haven't done it yet?"

Questions were racing through my mind, and Tami didn't understand what was happening to me. "Rachel," she said. "Are you all right?" She had no idea what was happening to me beneath the surface.

"No, everything is not all right, Tami, not at all!" I wanted to shout, but instead I said, "Yes, everything's fine, I just can't believe that she is going to become a Jew!" Actually, the big surprise was occurring inside of me: without any warning, the truth of the matter had tapped me on my shoulder, and I realized that I had not kept my promise. That discovery left me no rest. I knew that it wasn't enough to just "believe" in Hashem; our religion requires action.

After I finished work, I returned to my apartment outside Jerusalem. It was a warm summer day, but my apartment was cool. The shutters were closed in two of the rooms, keeping out the heat. After I settled myself in and ate something, I felt refreshed and decided to devote the rest of the day to laundry and housecleaning. My roommate wasn't home since she worked the night shift.

I finished my work and sat down on my bed to fold the laundry.

A hundred thoughts were nagging at me. I got up from my bed and stood to look out the window. A tree growing near my window blocked my view of the sky, but I managed to glimpse some blue between the branches.

My thoughts automatically returned to the Arab woman. "An Arab woman wants to become a Jew, but what about me?" I was lucky enough to be born with a Jewish *neshamah*, yet I was not performing too many of Hashem's mitzvot. I wanted to perform more mitzvot, and I realized that I hadn't done it until now because I was afraid.

A full week of consideration after my encounter with the Arab woman led me to a fork in the road. I knew that if I chose the high road, I would find peace. I'd been running all my life, or rather, I'd been trying to escape the pain all my life, but now I'd finally arrived at the crucial point where I had to make a decision.

For years, I'd been pushing away my feelings, but now they'd finally come out. I knew this was an essential step toward healing myself completely.

When I finally digested this new reality, a great cry rose up inside of me. Tears poured down my face as I wondered, *What am I supposed to do now? Where can I go?* I realized there was no place to turn except to the One Who sat on High. If I'd run to Him and pour out my pain, I knew that He would help me. He'd been waiting so long for me, and He was still waiting.

I listened carefully to hear the small voice inside of me, and it said, "You've had so much pain and turmoil for so many years, and now you've reached a turning point. You can see now that you've been paralyzed by fear. But now the time has come! You aren't seven years old anymore; you are twenty-three, no longer a child. You've matured. Your insights have deepened. This is the true test."

I knew that I wanted to make a change, to live differently, and for the first time, I stood and asked the One Who runs the world: *Which path should I take? What's my next step?* I knew that the next step I'd take would lead me toward the peace I sought so desperately.

I had guarded my promise for sixteen years. For sixteen years, I'd been merely surviving instead of living. I was afraid that if my internal pillar was ever taken from me, I would disappear, with no identity, no parents, and no purpose.

Not anymore! I decided finally to express what was in my heart, and by this, I mean my faith and trust in Hashem. This was what had been hidden deep inside since I was a child, but to my regret, I had never allowed it to emerge. I understood that true belief in Hashem required performance of His mitzvot, yet I was afraid that I would be judged and found wanting, and again, my Judaism would be questioned. I feared that perhaps I would make a mistake or sin inadvertently, and I would again suffer, and again they would point an accusing finger at me, so I decided to refrain from my desire and remain inconspicuous so I wouldn't have to deal with any of it. Now the time had come for me to decide once and for all: Am I a full-fledged Jew who is ready to take on the struggle, or G-d forbid the opposite… And so, I chose the path that was tried and true. I didn't care what people thought of me and how they saw me. My faith and trust in Hashem could never be taken away from me, by anyone! I parted once and for all from the doubt that had followed me and sent it on its way, away from me.

Mitzllal had reminded me of my doubted identity, and I had chosen to disconnect from her, even though Mitzllal had faith and trust and so many gifts. I now clung to Mitzllal and to all that had happened in the past, and I decided to take the positive things along with me: the faith and trust in myself and my identity, and my faith in Hashem.

I decided to go in the way of the Torah, with faith and trust and without fear, and leave no room for doubt and other harmful things. In the light of this milestone, I set out on my new path.

Returning

So many people are afraid to embark,
To return to Hashem with all of their heart.
They avoid returning to Hashem,
Afraid of what others will say about them.
Perhaps they question their purpose and goals,
But prefer a life filled with deep gaping holes.
They fear missing out, and so many changes,
They're afraid to look odd and be laughed at by strangers.
But if they ignore the fear and the shame,
And dare to approach the Holiest Name,
They will certainly merit help from on High,
And He will greet them with mercy, Hashem *Elokai*.
With love and with warmth, He will gather them in,
And help them to travel His path, to begin.
And they, who have opened the tiniest space
Will travel His path at their own special pace.

At the start of my journey, I penned a letter to myself expressing my feelings. I wrote: *I believe in You,* Ribono Shel Olam; *everything is from You, and it is all good, and I know that the day will come when I will bond with You and build my own Jewish home. I am hiding the*

The Arab Messenger

tempest of my heart in this little note, and thus, from now on, I will feel that Hashem sees my distress, and He will extend His hand to help me.

I started attending Torah classes. Even if I'd be exhausted after work, I would go anyway. I drank the words thirstily. Tami was thrilled and took me along to classes and lectures. I started to observe mitzvot I hadn't observed before. At first, I was racing to catch up on all that I had missed; I wanted to do everything to perfection, and I was disappointed when I couldn't take it all on at once. I soon realized that I had to slow down. I decided to take on one mitzvah at a time, and once I got used to it, I would take on another. I grew closer than ever to Hashem, and I felt exhilarated, and the light spread to those who loved me the most.

My parents were thrilled when they saw their long-lost Mitzllal return home. One Friday evening, I went with my mother to the *beit haknesset*. Ima always went to pray there, but this time was special for both of us. I felt like laughing and crying simultaneously. There were many women sitting in the women's section. They stood when they needed to stand, they sat when they needed to sit, they moved their hands forward and gestured, murmuring prayers on their lips, but they couldn't read a single letter of the siddur. I was the only one there who knew how to read. I felt like crying for them, because they couldn't read or write, and for myself, because with all of my abilities, I had not used them for prayer. At the same time, I was proud of my mother and all the other women who gathered there and prayed so devoutly in their own way. The mouth doesn't need a siddur in order to pray.

Sixteen years of unrest and struggle had finally come to an end; a ceasefire had finally been called. I understood that Mitzllal would always live inside of me, and erasing her name on my identity card had accomplished nothing. Mitzllal was still hurting, sore, and insulted over the doubt placed on her identity, and Rachel was trying to live in the present, to overcome those feelings and bring the two of them to acknowledge their value. I had to make a balance between them.

The first step was learning how to do that.

CHAPTER TWENTY-EIGHT

Thoughts of Home

My return to Torah Judaism was a time of tremendous growth and rejuvenation for me. Even though I had never strayed very far from observance, I had always been drawn to it and was always looking for more. So many new things were going on around and inside of me. My attitude changed remarkably, replacing my painful past with living in the present and planning the future. My vision sharpened and expanded, and I started to set goals for myself that would lead me to my true purpose in life. I began to think about finding a suitable husband, getting married, and building my own home. I knew exactly what kind of man I wanted to share my life with. The picture I had in my mind was completely different from what I would have wanted in the past.

Marrying a man who was not Ethiopian was out of the question. I was looking for someone who could identify with me, who could travel back in time with me to our shared experiences. Anyone other than an Ethiopian man would not be able understand what I went through. He would want to move forward and never look back, without comprehending my pain. Marriage to a non-Ethiopian would sweep my past under the rug forever. It was so complex, and so important; how could I possibly disregard it?

Despite my strong feelings on the subject, the One Above had other plans. The *Ribono Shel Olam* didn't want me to hold on to my anger and bitterness toward the ones who had hurt me. Rather, He wanted me to get rid of those feelings and replace them with love, respect, and faith in other Jews, even if they weren't similar to me externally. He wanted me to learn to love them and connect with them the way I had wanted to when I was a child. He wanted me to join hands with them and move forward in true unity. He knew that this was what I had been looking for ever since I was a child. The *Ribono Shel Olam* wanted me to close an old circle and open a new one, exactly as I had dreamed when I was young.

My husband Akiva's nature was strong and solid, and it helped us build a stable and impregnable relationship. I could see the truth in him. I had been raised with this sort of stability in my parents' home. I was always searching for the pure, straightforward, and unadulterated truth in Hashem's world, and I always found it. It does exist, if only on rare occasions.

Rav Kook writes, "When the spirit shines, even foggy skies make pleasant light." When I started to grow in my Torah observance, my *neshamah*, shrouded in fog for so long, threw it off, and in its place came a powerful light. I met Akiva while I was basking in this light. From the moment we met, I felt as though I knew him. I didn't understand how this could be possible, but today I know that it was because he and I were so incredibly alike. I saw that he had the same solid values of truth, purity, and integrity as I did. With Hashem's help, we prepared to get married and start building a home together. We focused on the essentials only and avoided getting bogged down by unimportant things. We knew that it would be difficult for people to accept us, even though it is wrong to judge others by how they look rather than by who they are. Akiva and I were two Jews, children of Avraham, Yitzchak and Yaakov, with no differences or barriers between us.

CHAPTER TWENTY-NINE

The Sound of Joy and Celebration

Hearts full of happiness, we set a date for our *chatunah*. We were so excited when the time came to go to the Rabbanut and arrange our marriage license and *ketubah*. The *rav* welcomed us and started asking us all the necessary questions. When it came to the part where it said "Rachel *bat*…" I gave him the name of my father, Yosef. "True," the *rav* said, "but since you underwent *giyur l'chumrah* (immersion into the *mikvah* due to the "questionable status"), we'll write *bat* Avraham Avinu."

I was devastated. After I had finally connected to Hashem, they took my birth father away from me! I tried to stop my tears from falling, but it was impossible, so I stood up and walked out of the office. Through my tear-filled eyes, I saw the image of my parents in my mind, standing there in the corner of the room, and right before my eyes, my father started to shrink until there was nothing left of him. In his place, a clever little boy appeared who, already at three years of age, knew there was a Creator. I saw him drawing people away from their mistaken beliefs and teaching them to know and love Hashem. I could see the difficult tests that Avraham Avinu faced and triumphed over, but even so, I was distraught by the fact that my parents' memory was being "erased," so to speak.

I was lucky to have had a very good upbringing, based on uncompromising allegiance to the truth. My parents' warm hearts spilled over like "oil running down the beard of Aharon." They were so pure and wholehearted in everything they did, and their faith in *Hakadosh Baruch Hu* was always steady and immovable.

Whenever I told my mother about something that hurt me, she would say, "Why do you care about what people say? You should just be careful about what comes out of your own mouth." Then she would add, "You heard something? Pretend you didn't hear it. You saw something? Pretend you didn't see it."

When we would want something that one of the neighbors had, she would say, "Why do you care about what they have? Look at what *you* have!" My parents taught us to be happy with what we had and how important it was to guard our tongues and never hurt anyone. These basic principles were the foundation that my siblings and myself were formed upon, and we grew into people with integrity and good *middot*.

I could see my mother now in my mind's eye, and I realized there was one thing that I hadn't taken with me. How was it possible that I forgot the most important principle she taught us? My mother had always told us to listen to our inner selves when it came to the right thing to say and do. I hadn't listened to my mother when she said, "Why do you care about what others say? You keep doing what you have to do." My mother knew that working on ourselves and monitoring our own behavior was the best way to serve Hashem.

When I shared with my mother how I felt about the *safek*, she said to me, as was her way, "Why do you care about what they say? Jewish, not Jewish… With doubt, without doubt… You keep doing what you have to do." But I had veered off the right path and continued carrying the *safek* and all its implications on my back. I had placed so much weight on the *safek* that it had almost knocked me down. I wasted so many years worrying about it, and even now, right before my *chatunah*,

The Sound of Joy and Celebration

it was trying to draw me back in, taunting me, "Now we are taking your father and mother away from you right in front of your eyes!"

Never again! I told myself. At that moment, I decided to return to the path my mother had paved for me. I knew how much she worried about me when she saw me asking and probing and worrying about my identity, afraid that it would drive me out of my mind, G-d forbid. I had wasted so many years, but it was never too late. Then, before my *chatunah*, I was compelled to go back and figure out why I was so troubled by it so that I could relax, move on with my life, and follow in my mother's footsteps.

The corner where I had imagined my mother standing was empty now, and as I was trying to calm down, my *chatan* came out to me. "I understand how you're feeling," he said, trying to comfort me.

"Thank you for understanding," I replied. "I just need a little more time to myself right now." He nodded and went back into the office.

I tried to make sense of the pictures I'd seen: My father standing in the corner, getting smaller and smaller until he faded away, and how Avraham Avinu had taken his place. Then I'd seen my mother and the wonderful *chinuch* she'd given us. They had brought us up to be good, honest people, but Avraham Avinu was also my father, as was Hashem. It was a source of pride for me, and I decided that I should be happy with what I had. What was written on the form made no difference—I was connected to all of them!

I returned to the office and sat down again, this time without tears, but with acceptance. The *rav*, seeing that my eyes were red from crying, turned to me and said, "I'm so sorry to see you like this."

"I'm all right now," I replied. "I just needed to be alone for a few minutes."

This incident taught me that I should be thankful that I am a descendant of Avraham Avinu, one of the pillars of the world, and that I should also be thankful to my parents for all that they did for me.

My wedding day finally arrived, and it was a special evening for a special couple. Ethiopian and Ashkenazic/chassidic music blended together to mark the uniqueness of the occasion. The wedding hall was shining with a new light. A new chapter was opening in my life.

CHAPTER THIRTY

Tried and Tested in America

When Akiva and I decided to get married, I had one condition: that we live in Eretz Yisrael and raise our children there. If the saying of *Chazal*, "*Eretz Yisrael nikneh b'yissurim*—Eretz Yisrael is acquired through suffering," applied to anyone, it was me, and after all I had been through, I was not willing to give it up. Eretz Yisrael was my home. My husband tried to entice me with promises of physical comfort, but I knew this was a test. I told him I was willing to sacrifice everything—I would even live in a tent—in order to remain in Eretz Yisrael. Once my husband saw how serious I was about this, he agreed to my request. He only asked that we go back to America for a short time so that he could close up the law office he shared with his father.

For the year and a half we spent in the States, my husband hoped that I would be won over by the comfortable American lifestyle he was providing for me. I, however, was determined to make our stay in America temporary, so when we settled into our new home, we each had a different outcome in mind. Akiva was hoping the move would become permanent while I was anxious to return home as soon as possible. I was starving for *ruchniyut*, spiritual growth; all I wanted was to learn and grow in Torah.

Our house was a ten-minute walk from my in-laws', so we were able to visit them fairly easily. My mother-in-law worked very hard to make me happy and keep me occupied until my husband would return home from work, and we became much more than daughter- and mother-in-law—a warm friendship grew between us. She would tell me stories of my husband's childhood, and through these stories, I came to know him better.

My husband and his father would leave for work very early in the morning and return home late in the evening. We ate dinner together, sometimes at home and sometimes at my in-laws' house. He would tell me about his day and all the clients who came in to see him, and he'd ask me about how I spent my day. He was very relieved when he realized how much I enjoyed spending time with his mother.

Besides his work schedule, my husband also set aside time to learn after Shacharit. He occasionally went out in the evening to learn, as well. We also learned together, but after I while, I felt my spiritual level starting to decline. I had stopped *davening*, for example. When I told my husband how I was feeling, he encouraged me to start again, knowing how much I had enjoyed *tefillah*. It worked for a while, but I stopped again shortly thereafter.

One day, Akiva returned home from Ma'ariv and told me that there was a *rav* visiting from Eretz Yisrael who was staying with one of our neighbors. I felt a need to speak to him about what was happening to me. I went to see him, and in tears, I explained how much my *ruchniyut* had been weakened since we had come to America, and I told him that it had reached the point where I was no longer *davening*.

The *rav* listened sympathetically, but then explained, "This is how it is in America. The *gashmiyut*, the materialism, seeps in, even through cracks in the windows. You just need to be strong, and I give you a *brachah*, a blessing, that you should pass the test!"

Tried and Tested in America

The *rav* helped me to understand that it was the exposure to materialism that was siphoning away parts of my spirituality. Whenever I found myself stumbling, all I had to do was look at what was in front of me—materialism or spirituality—in order to make the right decisions.

Occasionally, I would join my husband at his office to get an idea of what he did for his *parnassah*. I met the lovely people who worked there, and I particularly enjoyed the company of the secretary who had been employed by my father-in-law for more than fifty years and had become part of the family. I met some of Akiva's clients, and I tried to pitch in wherever I could.

The *rav's* words—about materialism pushing away spirituality—weighed heavily upon me. I wanted to build a house of Torah and was willing to do anything to achieve that goal, but the reality was that my husband spent most of his time working at his law office.

I admired his dedication to his work, but I wanted for him to have a chance to explore his spiritual side, as well. From the first time we met, I could see how spiritually powerful he was, but I could also see that he had no way of expressing it. I believed that with time and patience, it would transform from potential to actuality.

Meanwhile, our beautiful daughter was born, filling our home with light, warmth, and love. I worked very hard to be the best wife and mother I could possibly be. Akiva was also working very hard to make life as pleasant and comfortable as possible, hoping that I would want to stay in America, so he was very surprised when I approached him one day and told him that I wanted to go home.

Akiva couldn't believe that I was willing to give up the wonderful life he was offering me to live in Eretz Yisrael. I explained to him that from the time I was four years old, I never asked for anything and I never complained of hunger or thirst. All I wanted was spirituality, and the American materialism was pulling it away from me, and that was something I wouldn't stand for at any price.

It took two more months for Akiva to close down the family business. We boarded the plane and returned to our real home. My daughter Moriah slept peacefully in my arms, safe and secure. In stark contrast to my happiness, Akiva was still in shock as he left everything behind and headed into uncharted territory.

CHAPTER THIRTY-ONE

Eretz Yisrael Is Our Home!

Upon our return, there was no shortage of challenges lying in wait for us, and some of them were really hard to conquer. The transition from America to Eretz Yisrael was very difficult for Akiva. We lived in my in-laws' apartment in Beitar Illit for about four months. Akiva's sister also lived nearby, and while I enjoyed meeting everyone and being a part of the family, we didn't really find our place there, so we moved to Yerushalayim.

Akiva, accustomed to working most of the day, now spent that time learning Torah. The drastic change was hard for him to adjust to, and he could not shake the obligation he felt to work and support our family, so he went to work in an orphanage. The work gave him tremendous satisfaction. He liked kids and was wonderful with them, and they loved him in return, so much so that a few of them are still in touch with him until today, but it still wasn't enough. Akiva missed living in America; his parents and grandparents lived there, and he felt he belonged there, with them. With time, though, these feelings faded and were replaced by involvement in the community and a search for a *rav*. The birth of our first son pushed everything back for a while as we basked in the presence of this beloved new family member.

After a year in Yerushalayim, Akiva still did not feel settled. We moved to Ramat Beit Shemesh, and it was there that my husband's restless soul found all it had been seeking: a wonderful community and a *rav* he respected and could rely on. My husband thrived, and we along with him.

It is so clear to us now that Hashem had sent us specifically to this neighborhood and gave us amazing neighbors who were not afraid of standing up for the truth and helping us in times of need.

My daughter Moriah was turning six at that time and was about to enter first grade. We were waiting anxiously to hear whether she was accepted into the school we had applied to. We had already been through this before when we were applying for kindergarten, and again, we were left wondering whether the reply would be positive or negative.

Even when my husband told me that she had been accepted, I knew I wouldn't relax until I saw her walking into that classroom and sitting down at a desk among the other girls in the class.

When Registration Day arrived, my daughter and I set out for the school. I could see her glowing face out of the corner of my eye as she skipped along beside me. My daughter was a lively, happy girl who was looking forward to a new beginning, exactly as I had at her age. Now I was paralyzed with fear, with no idea how my legs were not collapsing from under me as I walked. I was terrified that my daughter was going to experience the crushing disappointments I had gone through. If she wouldn't be accepted, what was I supposed to tell my darling daughter? How would I explain to her that she couldn't go to school because her mother was *safek Yehudi*?

I stepped into the office, trembling with fear. I couldn't stop the tears from falling, and my daughter was bewildered, wondering why her mother was crying. After the interview was over, I said to the principal, "If there's anything I need to change or fix, please tell me. I'll do anything that's necessary to help my daughter succeed."

She waved my doubts away, saying, "Don't worry, your daughter is with us!"

We left the school, tears still in my eyes, and headed for home. On the way, Moriah asked me why I was crying. How could I explain it to her?

"I'm excited," I said. "I'm thrilled that you are going up to *Kitah Aleph*! I remember being your age, and now you are so grown up and starting school! Remember how much you were looking forward to it?" I asked. Moriah nodded her head and smiled.

Of course, I'd only given her half an answer. How could I tell my daughter that I'd been afraid she would not be accepted? I remembered myself at that age; I'd been lively, smart, and mature for my age. I'd been so happy when I started school, until the *safek* started gnawing away at me, and that's when my exuberance disappeared, never to return. How could I tell my daughter about Mitzllal, that seven-year-old girl who had vanished from my life?

Today, my daughter is happily learning in the school we chose for her and is doing well. I give my thanks to the *Ribono Shel Olam* Who had sent us such faithful messengers who had accepted my children into the schools that were best for them.

I also must thank the messengers themselves. Their reward is without measure. I am learning Torah along with my children. Their *divrei Torah* seep inside of me and salve my wounds. These messengers can't begin to grasp the depth of my gratitude; only Hashem can fathom my joy, and surely He will repay them measure for measure for all the good they have done on our behalf.

CHAPTER THIRTY-TWO

Challenges

It's human nature to be curious, even though curiosity sometimes transcends the boundaries of good taste. People become especially curious when they see something that, to them, is out of ordinary. In our case, there was exceptional interest in an Ashkenazi Jew married to an Ethiopian.

"Akiva, you're a lawyer. You have everything going for you. Why did you marry her? Why did you do this to yourself?" Akiva was asked. I was furious the first time he told me about it, ready to vocally defend myself and my family, but after giving it some thought, I decided to take a different approach: say nothing. When it happened again two years later, I did the same, choosing to ignore it and continue working on myself. It saddened me that people could be so superficial. Was this our way, to look only at the outside and not at what's inside? It's impossible to judge a person only by what you see with your eyes; you have to look deeper and find out what is in that person's heart. Sadly, there aren't many who take this view. I chose to learn from the exalted *middot* of Hashem, raise myself to a higher level, and refrain from responding.

✶✶✶

"*Baruch Hashem*, G.'s son was accepted into the Talmud Torah," Akiva informed me. "*B'ezrat Hashem*, he'll be joining all the other boys who had started at the beginning of the year." I was happy to hear the good news and praised my husband for his role in it.

Challenges

We had already had some unpleasant experiences when trying to register our children for *cheder*, and after we had finally cleared all the obstacles, we decided to help other people with similar issues. My husband told me about many kids who weren't accepted into schools, and I encouraged him to advocate on their behalf. These families thought the sun rose and set on my husband, that he was sent to them from Heaven to help them with their difficulties. It helped my husband firmly establish himself as a leader in the community. The transition from America to Eretz Yisrael, from busy lawyer to *avreich*, had not been easy, and now he had finally found his place by helping others.

One day, I returned home from the playground boiling mad. "Did they call the kids '*kushi*' again?" asked my husband, seeing how angry I was.

"No," I said, "I'm already used to that." Then I asked him, "Akiva, do you have a few minutes to give me your undivided attention? I want to feel like you're listening to me and not standing with one foot out the door."

He sat down and gave me his full attention.

"While I was at the park," I began, "Mrs. P. was talking about an Ethiopian man who learns with her father-in-law; he's a very nice man, but not Jewish. Since the subject had come up, she asked me when I came to Eretz Yisrael, and I told her that we arrived 1983. I knew exactly where she was going with her questions. 'Did you have to *toivel* when you got here?' she asked. I answered, 'Yes,' knowing I had nothing to hide, and I also told her that I had to *toivel* again before my wedding. So Mrs. P. says, 'Right, the *tevilah* you did as a child has to be repeated when you're older, but did you know that from the moment you *toiveled*, your parents weren't your parents anymore?"

I finished speaking and took a deep breath. "How did she have the nerve to say that to me?" I asked, tears stinging my eyes. "Do I have the words 'NO FEELINGS' written in big letters on my forehead? Must she tell me every single thing that comes into her mind without thinking first?!"

It took Akiva a minute to understand my anger. Then he said, "Don't let that woman bring you down to her level. Those words are coming from her own pain and have nothing to do with you. Don't let her get under your skin and take you back to where you were."

Just then, my mother called. After exchanging greetings, I decided to tell her what had happened to me that day. "It's all because of this *safek*; it follows me wherever I go!" I said, tears welling up in my eyes again.

My mother responded exactly as my husband had: "Don't let it bother you. Just keep doing what you have to do."

Her words brought me back to my childhood home where they were a constant refrain. I'd grown up in the shadow of these words, but for some reason, I couldn't internalize them. Only now, married and more mature, did they finally start to take root in my heart. I had to let my inner truth guide me and avoid getting distracted by what other people thought about me. I had to continue to work on myself and not get sidetracked by others' opinions. But how could I change directions so abruptly after so much time? The change had to come, but when was it going to start?

"*Make for Me an opening the size of a needle, and I will make for you an opening the size of a wedding hall.*" Only *Hakadosh Baruch Hu*, Who saw my desire to grow, offered me His help and lit the way for me, so that I could find my way out from this seemingly endless tunnel.

CHAPTER THIRTY-THREE

The End of an Era

Saba Getahun, my paternal grandfather, made *aliyah* in 5750 (1990). The rest of the family had all come before he did and were waiting impatiently for him to leave Ethiopia and move to Eretz Yisrael. When I saw him after his arrival, I was greeted by a strong and dignified man who had fought in the war between the Democrats and the Communists. We grandchildren only vaguely remembered him from Ethiopia, and along with our parents, aunts, and uncles, were barely able to contain our excitement when he finally arrived. Our first meeting with him was a little awkward since we didn't know him so well, but Saba immediately put us at ease. He had a wonderful sense of humor, and in no time at all, he had us all laughing, transforming the atmosphere from strained to sweet.

Eventually, we grew to know him very well (while we had never even seen a picture of my maternal grandfather). He was very independent, cooking his own meals and washing and ironing his clothing, and he was always very well groomed. We loved and admired him, and when we sat around his table, he would keep us enthralled with heroic tales of war, courage, and tenacity, peppered with his trademark sense of humor.

The last time I saw him was when he came to spend Shabbat at the home of my parents. Saba didn't join us at the *seudah* as he usually did; he didn't eat and didn't tell stories about Ethiopia. Instead, he sat quietly and gazed at us. His behavior was out of character and a harbinger of things to come.

Saba had been waiting for two months for his nephew's wedding date to arrive, but on that day, we were informed that he wasn't feeling well and would be staying home. Abba, who knew very well how much his father had been looking forward to the *chatunah,* understood immediately that if his father was missing out on it, he must be feeling terrible. He quickly went to Saba's home, and his worst fears were realized when Saba asked Abba to take him to the hospital.

On the way, Saba poured his heart out to his son, speaking with him and blessing him. It was as if he knew his end was near and decided to take advantage of the moment to offer some parting words.

A few minutes after they arrived at the hospital, Saba lost consciousness and was placed on a respirator.

After Shabbat was over, my mother told me of my grandfather's worsening condition and started to prepare me for what would happen in the coming days. The doctors were saying that Saba had one or two days left to live, and being Ethiopians, we liked to be prepared in advance for these types of situations, but when my mother tried to speak to me about it, I didn't want to hear it.

Even so, I realized that I shouldn't delay going to visit Saba in the hospital, in case it would be too late. I went first to Kiryat Gat to pick up my sister Elisheva, and together, we traveled to Soroka Medical Center in Be'er Sheva. We went up to Saba's room and found Abba sitting beside his bed, saying Tehillim. It was painful to see him hooked up to the respirator, unable to see us or hear us, his legs swollen to twice their size. I had seen him so recently hale and hearty despite his eighty-seven years, and now he looked so old and frail. I leaned over and kissed him on the forehead and told him, "Don't worry, Saba, everything will be all right." I left the room while Elisheva stayed to say Tehillim.

Abba and I spoke to the doctor, who told us that Saba had hours to live, not days, as they had told us previously. While we were sitting in his office, we heard shouting from the hallway. A nurse opened the door and asked the doctor to come to Saba's room. He ran to the room and closed the door behind him. Moments later, the tumult stopped, and there was silence. Saba had passed away. It was Sunday, 14 Shevat, 5765 (January 21, 2008).

Abba howled in sorrow, and we held his hands and cried with him. I would miss Saba, his presence and his stories. He was the last remnant of my past and the only one who could help me resolve the nagging question of my identity. From then on, I would have to deal with the *safek* all by myself.

As the days passed, I couldn't reconcile myself to Saba's death. All the memories I had of him were joyful. I asked myself why I had said to Saba that "everything would be all right." Why didn't I say, "Don't worry, Saba, you'll get better"? After giving it some thought, I realized that Saba had known of my struggle, and he'd been waiting for me to tell him, "I will be all right. I will figure it out." Once he'd heard me say these words, his soul was able to rest. An hour after I spoke them, Saba's *neshamah* quietly returned to the *Borei Olam*.

CHAPTER THIRTY-FOUR

Awakenings

One day, a magazine headline caught my eye. Spelled out in huge letters on the cover, it read: "*Shachor B'einayim*" (literally "black in the eyes"), a play on words to describe the dark Israeli nightmare that would be expected to occur if candidate Barack Obama would be elected president of the United States.

Those two words, spread out over an entire page, had a bad connotation to me, and I couldn't get them out of my mind. I paged through the magazine until I found the article, and then read it carefully. By the time I was finished, I realized that the fact that he was running for president wasn't the point of the article; the issue was that he was tied to figures in the Muslim world. The article also implied that the secret to Obama's success was that his mother was white, as if to say that a black person had no chance to succeed.

I was deeply insulted by the insinuations made in the article. I asked myself, "What would have happened if my children would know how to read, and they would have seen an article like this?" I was grateful they couldn't read or write yet, and I put the magazine somewhere where they couldn't get to it.

When my husband came home after his learning *seder*, I showed him the article. When he finished reading it, I asked him, "Am I right in thinking that their problem with Obama is his skin color, or am I just being oversensitive because of my experiences when I was younger? If the children would know how to read, do you think they would understand what the writer was trying to say?" Akiva agreed with me, then put the magazine back where I'd left it. "Let's sleep on it. We'll talk more about it tomorrow," he said. "Don't let it bother you."

But I couldn't fall asleep. I tiptoed out of the room, sat down, and wrote a response to the article, protesting to the way they had presented their facts. The next day, I typed it up and sent it off to the editor. Immediately I felt better; somehow, the act of protesting a perceived injustice was enough to calm me down.

A while later, I noticed another headline: "Barack Obama as an Example." The article expressed great surprise over how a black man actually became president of the United States, and how unusual it was for someone who had such limited opportunities to overcome the hurdles in his way and succeed beyond anyone's expectations. It was actually very inspiring, but I was struck by the irony: the author was noting how an American black overcame tremendous prejudice and obstacles in order to arrive at where he was today...while ignoring the great prejudice that exists in our very own Jewish community! And so I found myself writing another letter to the editor.

Barack Obama's story, I wrote, *is indeed fascinating and inspiring, but I find it surprising that you need to look so far beyond our own community to find someone to admire. We are so fortunate to be living in Eretz Hakodesh, and as opposed to different eras of the past, we are permitted to keep the Torah and mitzvot freely. It is mystifying to me why, when we are blessed with such freedom, we create our own obstacles.*

We don't need to look as far back as fifty years to the prejudice that had existed then against "kushim" when the situation still exists today. If back then there were segregated buses, today we can speak about the division between the Ashkenazim and the Sephardim.

If America, the land of the non-Jews, can manage to overcome their prejudice and let a black man lead them, then surely we can overcome ours as well. The status quo can be changed if we want it that way. Those who are listening can hear the silent scream ringing out amid the din: "We want change!" In order to merit it, we must daven, "Enlighten our eyes with Your Torah, focus our minds on Your mitzvot, unite our hearts in love and reverence for Your Name…" *so that we may* "…rejoice in Your salvation."

Indeed, Barack Obama is an amazing role model, but we need to do a lot more than sit around and sing his praises. May we merit to change what needs to be changed and to fix what is broken, so that we can stand together as one nation united. "Fortunate are you, righteous ones, you who exert yourselves in Torah, and you who fear G-d, for there is a hidden, concealed, and protected place for you in Gan Eden in the future."

With blessing,
Rachel L., Ramat Beit Shemesh

I saw the fact that I wasn't afraid to draw attention to myself and express my thoughts and feelings as real progress in my personal development. The little girl of twenty-five years earlier was finally getting a chance to speak her mind.

Not long afterward, I took my son for a check-up at the local clinic. When it was my turn, the nurse came out of the office and called out, "Lebowitz." Upon hearing my name, I stood up and went into the examining room. The nurse took down my information and we got to chatting a bit. She was curious about an Ethiopian woman with an Ashkenazi name, and she asked me where my children went to school, well aware that it was not easy to be accepted into the better schools in the neighborhood. I answered her questions, then asked her where her children learned.

She told me about the struggles people were having in her neighborhood. "Three people I know changed their family names so that they would be accepted in schools," she said.

I nodded sadly and said, "They changed their entire identity for the sake of somebody's acceptance? Is that what Hashem wants from us, to throw away a name that was passed down through generations and take on another identity? I'm sure if they could change the color of their skin, they would do that, too," I said.

The nurse continued, "When they were discovered, their children were thrown out of the Ashkenazi schools."

Stories like these were disturbing because they reminded me that I, too, had tried to disconnect from my identity: I had erased my Ethiopian name and I distanced myself from traditional Ethiopian food and anything else that reminded me of my past—much to my sorrow. It was painful to see other people making the same mistake that I had made.

I recalled my friend Yehudit's request to explain the pain I was feeling. That evening, after Akiva went out to learn, I sat down on the couch, lost in my thoughts, and my gaze was drawn to a photograph of a little curly-haired girl, dressed in her white *zuryah* (cotton dress) embroidered in red, yellow, and green. The picture stood on a shelf among the *sifrei kodesh*. The girl's eyes were sparkling, and her face was radiant.

"Tell me, *yaldah* (little girl). How did we survive all these challenges? How can I get rid of the pain this *safek* is causing me? Mitzllal, please tell me, how can I get past it?"

I stared at the picture until she answered me from wherever she was: "Just as my picture is standing among the *sifrei kodesh*, you, too, are standing among your brethren in Eretz Yisrael, the Land of Our Fathers. You see the special light shining out from me? You can also have this light if you keep staying on the path of Torah. If you can do that, you will be stronger than ever!"

This was a very special moment for me. I felt calm and relaxed, and a powerful connection arose between that little girl in the picture and the wife and mother sitting on the couch. Rachel and Mitzllal had finally found each other. They mourned the lost years, rejoiced in their reunion, yet cried over all that had happened.

This reunion provided me with some new perspectives.

"I know, *yaldah*, how you looked forward to finding *achdut*, unity; I know how long you have been waiting for this moment and how much energy you have invested while you were working toward this picture of *achdut*. And I know, *yaldah*, how disappointed you were. Your dream of *achdut* was shattered, and I know that was not what you dreamed of.

"I will comfort you by saying, 'Don't worry. Your dream will yet come true; I promise you!' It was no childish dream you had; it is the same dream that every Jew has, from the oldest to the youngest. Everyone is waiting for *achdut*, and I promise you that I will continue to hope and wait for that day to come. And this time, I know that I won't be disappointed. That day is yet to come."

I imagined a clean white page spread out in front of me. I was holding a paintbrush in my hand, drawing a clear blue sky, with no clouds or fog obscuring it. There is no rainbow (*keshet*—קשת) in my sky, no prism of colors that indicate jealousy (*kinah*), hatred (*sinah*), and competition (*tacharut*), which correspond to its letters. All will be light and clear. The yellow sun will send out its rays, enveloping all of Klal Yisrael with warmth, love, and *achdut* when each of us will take upon him- or herself the yoke of Heaven.

"Yes, *yaldah*, I will rise up for both of our sakes and try to contribute to the fulfillment of that vision in my own way, with hope and anticipation for that special day."

During this moment of epiphany, I heard a familiar voice calling my name. "Rachel, wake up. What are you dreaming about?" the voice asked.

My gaze turned from the picture of the little girl that stood on the bookshelf toward the voice calling me. "Shalom, Akiva," I answered, still immersed in my musings. My husband had been out learning for the past three hours and now found me sitting in the same position I had been before he left.

"What are you thinking about?" he asked again. "Is everything all right? Are you still thinking about the *safek*?" he asked, knowing that I had promised him I wouldn't let it bother me.

As he was waiting for me to answer, we suddenly heard a crash. His question hovered in the air as we ran toward the sound. My picture of the happy girl was lying amid shards of glass. The glass obscured the radiance that surrounded her. My gaze moved from the picture of the little girl to Akiva, and I answered, "I'm fine. Everything is fine. The *safek* is not going to bother me anymore."

"How'd you get to that?" he asked, knowing how disturbing I found the subject.

"It was a test sent to me to see how much *emunah* and *bitachon* I had in Hashem, and I just decided to get over it," I said to him, and I started to gather up the pieces of broken glass.

Akiva was happy to hear my reply and came over to help me. He picked up the picture in order to brush off the glass, but I stopped him. "I'll do it."

My husband watched me as I carefully brushed the glass from the girl's face until I could see its shine once more. A smile broke out on my face, and Akiva looked at me and asked, "What happened to you while I was gone tonight?"

"A lot!" I answered.

"*Kein yirbu*," my husband murmured and continued to sweep up the glass. Meanwhile, I looked for a new frame for the picture, and I found a gold frame that had been sitting in my closet for years. I slipped the picture into the new frame and put it on the middle shelf of the bookcase, but then moved it to the top shelf, where it looked perfect. The light that was radiating from the little girl's face joined the light from mine.

I told my husband that I was ready to move past the pain. I chose to live and not just survive. I would connect the final pieces of the puzzle and feel whole again. I chose to live with *emunah* and *bitachon* in Hashem without fear, and through this *bitachon*, I would reclaim the belief in myself that I had lost in my childhood.

In hindsight, I realize that the *safek* had left me dangling between two worlds. For many years, I was neither able to call myself a Jew who kept mitzvot in the fullest sense of the word, nor was I a Jew who didn't keep the mitzvot at all, so I was struggling with another *safek* as well. It is *forbidden* for a Jew to doubt himself. A Jew must know he is a Jew, and everyone around him must know it, too.

Why did I become *Chareidi* when they were the ones who threw my Judaism into doubt, especially when I wanted to distance myself from the *safek* so much? There are four words that dispel any doubt I may have had over my decision: "*Elokai Avraham, Yitzchak, v'Yaakov.*" I had been hearing these words for as long as I could remember when my mother murmured them after she lit the Shabbat candles, just before she made her requests. These words had lain dormant in my heart since my youth, but it was only now that I was really able to internalize them.

I remembered the turning point that caused me to alter my path. It was during a lull in the crowds that normally filled the bakery where I worked. I was sitting behind the counter, saying Tehillim. At this point, I was learning more and more about Dovid Hamelech, the author of the *Sefer Tehillim*. I would usually say Tehillim after I finished *davening* Shacharit until I arrived at school or work. I identified with Dovid Hamelech and the struggles that plagued him all his life.

While I was saying Tehillim that day, I noticed two *Chareidi* families who had come into the bakery. They were two married brothers with their families who had come for a special lunch or early supper. Something about them caught my attention, so I finished saying Tehillim and started to observe them.

The food was served at their table, and before they started eating, they all got up to wash their hands. They sat down, made some *brachot*, and started to eat. I was fascinated by the sight and couldn't take my eyes off them. When they finished, they said the Grace After Meals and stood to go. I followed them with my gaze as they left the bakery. I stood in my place behind the counter, replaying the whole scene in my mind, trying to figure out what it was about them that was so mesmerizing.

I had encountered *Chareidim* many times in the past, but now more than ever, the sight of them gave me pause. We inhabited two separate worlds. We all grew up in the same place, but the gap between us was enormous. I grew up in the State of Israel, but they grew up in Eretz Yisrael. These "two places" symbolized two completely separate paths, and the differences between them were like the differences between heaven and earth.

In my heart of hearts, I knew that their path was mine, as well, the one I really wanted to follow. At that point, I possessed tools I hadn't had in the past; I knew the language, and all I really needed to do was decide which path I wanted to take. The true path stood open in front of me, clear and shining.

For so many years, I had longed for true spirituality, but was afraid to make the change. The time had clearly arrived to take the first step. I left the State of Israel and entered the land *Hakadosh Baruch Hu* had promised to Avraham and all of his offspring.

The transition was not easy, but once I had made that decision, I realized that all the pain and struggle I had gone through over my identity had not been for nothing. In my effort to distance myself from the *safek*, I found a life completely *devoid* of doubt, the one true path of abundance, certainty, and safety. By following this path, I found the serenity, joy, and relief I had sought throughout the search for my identity.

Now, after eight years of living the *Chareidi* life I had chosen, I was still afraid of stumbling or making any sort of mistake that would thrust me back into that world of doubt. I was afraid to ask questions because I didn't want people to think I didn't belong.

However, after reconnecting to Mitzllal, I made the second transformation of my life. Instead of being afraid of people, a new fear entered me: fear of Hashem. I set out on my new path, at peace with the *psak halachah* that had been imposed upon me and with the *poskim* who had enforced it, but more important, I was finally at peace with my identity.

Today, I follow the rulings of the *gedolei hador* without question, and I educate my children in that way as well. "I have done complete *teshuvah* before Hashem," I declared to my husband.

CHAPTER THIRTY-FIVE

Descendants of Dan?

For many years I have gathered inspiration and encouragement from the writings of Eldad ha-Dani.

As I wrote earlier, Eldad ha-Dani was a traveling Jewish merchant who lived in the ninth century. After leaving Ethiopia during one of his travels, he circulated the news that the descendants of Dan and the rest of the ten tribes could be found in East Africa. He wrote about the decision of Shevet Dan not to fight their brethren, and how they had decided to find a new place to live in order to avoid fighting the war.

I am neither a scientist nor a researcher, and I don't have the tools to ascertain my origins, but I can identify completely with these words, and I'm certain that many Ethiopian Jews feel the same way.

The members of Shevet Dan didn't want to fight their brothers and spill their blood. They preferred to leave Eretz Yisrael and die elsewhere than fight their fellow Jews.

I had so many questions: After so many years of isolation and fear of war with their brothers, could they in fact be returning home? Were the Beta Yisrael descendants from that brave tribe who had endangered their lives rather than engaging in warfare with their brethren? Was this tribe now finding the same struggle awaiting them, as though the earlier conflict had happened just yesterday? We have no proof that we are actually descendants of this tribe that had feared spilling the blood of their brothers. But there is one thing of which I am certain: we have no interest in spilling blood. We left Ethiopia and came to Eretz Yisrael peacefully. It was painful to see the strife that existed among the Jews. After thousands of years of isolation, we had still not found that which we had been searching for: peace among brothers.

Would there ever be peace? I had been seeking *achdut* for years—*achdut* without barriers, without labels, hierarchy, or stigma. This *achdut* would express the common denominator among us all: we are Jews, and we are all children of *Hakadosh Baruch Hu*. We are all equal in His eyes, without any walls dividing us.

When I spoke with my sister Elisheva about this, she tried to explain to me that it was impossible for everyone to be equal and united. "Even at Kriat Yam Suf," she told me, "the sea divided into twelve paths, one for each tribe. You are dreaming a dream that could never come true. This is the way of the world; each group has its customs, each community its traditions. It would be impossible to unite everyone."

I did not agree with her. "There might be differences in the cultures or customs of different groups, and that's the beauty of Am Yisrael, but we're all brothers; we are all children of Avraham, Yitzchak, and Yaakov, and of course, *Hakadosh Baruch Hu*. Let's say there is a family of twelve children. Each child is different from the others, but they will always have one thing in common: they are all children of the same parents. There is much variety in Am Yisrael, but we're all children of Hashem. Is there anything better than coming together before Him with one voice, saying, 'Abba, we are Your children'?"

On Wednesday, Adar 15, 5769, I went with my family to pray at the gravesite of Dan ben Yaakov. I deeply identified with this tribe, and for the first time, I felt the need to pour out my heart in the place where my roots were presumed to lie. While my husband took the boys to the men's section, my daughter Moriah and I entered the women's section. Even though the room was empty, the candles burning on the table indicated that other women had been there before us. We closed our eyes and began to pray: "*Ribono Shel Olam*, we are turning to You after years of pain," I said. "When my identity was rejected, I was nearly destroyed. I am sure that You, too, were suffering. Please help us to find our lost brothers and join them, and this time, may the *achdut* be so strong that it should never be able to be extinguished. Please bring an end to this *galut* and all of our suffering."

CHAPTER THIRTY-SIX

Finding Inner Peace

Making peace with the past and reuniting Mitzllal and Rachel helped complete the missing pieces of the puzzle of my life. The two halves could not have been more different from each other, and yet, I was able to unite them through my strong connection with Hashem.

On Friday, Rosh Chodesh Iyar, 5770, I went with a group of women to Kever Rachel for the first time, where I *davened* an emotional and tear-stained *Shemoneh Esrei*. I felt every word speaking to me personally. After I finished, I opened my heart and listened, in my mind, to the prayers of Rachel Imeinu, crying for her children. I identified with her name and her pain. From the depths of my heart, I called to Hashem: "Abba! The righteous Rachel surely understands the depth of my pain, the pain of a small girl who waited with such anticipation to come to Eretz Yisrael, only to find *galut* here as well, and whose place among Am Yisrael was in doubt. I've been suffering for twenty-five years, and for Rachel Imeinu, it's been thousands of years. What's my pain compared to hers? Abba, You promised her that her children would return to their borders because You heard the sound of her crying, so I am turning to You with my request: please listen to her voice and give her the solace she asked for, so that all the tears that have been spilled here until now should join with hers, and that the suffering of her children should end."

Finding Inner Peace

At the *kever* of Rachel Imeinu, the mother of all Am Yisrael, I found the "Rachel" that was in me. My *tefillot* there connected me with both the name and the anguish we shared.

When I returned home, I felt like I'd been reborn, and I understood the important message that the *Ribono Shel Olam* wanted me to learn.

All my life, I'd been searching for proof of my identity, confirmation that would remove the *safek* that was pursuing me, but it had continued to elude me. It didn't exist, and the identity card I held in my hand was of no use. I understood that the only way a Jew could verify his authenticity was through his actions! This was the confirmation that would stand forever. I knew that there was one and only one proof of a Jew's identity, and it was not the card in my pocketbook.

The *Ribono Shel Olam*, by way of the search for my identity, wanted me to see the truth and not give up on it. Hashem gave me the test of the *safek* in order to see whether I would behave like a true Jewish woman. This was the test that was put before me and all the Beta Yisrael. We had been so happy to leave Ethiopia and rejoiced in our coming to Eretz Yisrael, and now all that was left for us to do was the will of Hashem.

Today, I understand that the *Ribono Shel Olam* orchestrated the events of my life, including my suffering, in order for me to grow. When I do the *ratzon* (will) of Hashem, I grow. Hashem was always with me, even when I was not with Him, throughout all my struggles, and He had never left me. He believed that I had the strength to overcome my challenges. I kept Him deep inside my heart, and He always came to my aid.

Today, I am going in the way of the Torah with faith and trust in Hashem. I am stronger than I have ever been, alive and thriving, relying on my trust.

Today, I am walking the path my mother laid out for me. I examine my actions and don't wait to catch the mistakes of others. I understand that in order to achieve *achdut*, I have to contribute my part in *avodat Hashem*. When each one of us does his or her part, we will be able to build true peace, and only then will the children of *Hakadosh Baruch Hu* be united as one with one heart.

I spent sixteen years of my life battling my reality, seeking a different one. Today, I understand that there was no point to this resistance—I had to accept reality as it was and see the good in it. I couldn't change the past, and I need to keep moving forward from wherever I am.

✳✳✳

One afternoon, I noticed a change in my son's behavior. I knew that something was bothering him, so I waited for the right moment to sit down and talk with him in his room. I asked him what was wrong, and he answered, in a weak and wounded tone, "Somebody called me '*kushi*'!"

"What does '*kushi*' mean?" I asked him.

"It means that I'm black," he replied.

"How do you feel about that?"

"Insulted."

"There are many different kinds of people," I explained to him. "There are people with blue eyes, people with brown eyes, and people with green eyes; people have either black hair, blond hair, or red hair; there are tall people and short people. Each person looks different from the other, but this is only what we see with our eyes.

"There's one thing they all have in common, though: they all have a *neshamah*, a part of Hashem, inside of them. Your *neshamah* is very pure and elevated. I am so proud of you and so happy that you are my son, and I love you very much," I said, giving him a hug. "You should know that all good things are hidden. Where do we keep the Torah?" I asked him.

"In the *aron kodesh*," he replied.

"And where is your *neshamah*?"

"Inside my body."

"That's right!" I said. "The things that can't be seen are the most important!"

I hugged him again and he ran off to play. After he was gone, I thought that my explanation might have been too lengthy for a six-year-old boy, and I didn't know whether he had absorbed what I had told him.

This is a poem that expressed my feelings:

There are two parts to every briah,
The physical body and the pure neshamah.
Joining together two halves of a whole,
Is the task Hashem has assigned to us all.
How can we pave the way to our goal?
By keeping the Torah—that is our role.
Body and soul bind together inside every Jew,
And finding the right balance is the task we must do.
Let's raise a prayer to our Father Above,
To give us wisdom, strength, and love.
And the soul should forever rule and succeed,
And b'ezrat Hashem *to our true purpose lead.*

Two weeks went by. During that time, I kept a close eye on my son's behavior, and I saw that he had gotten back to himself. One day, he came to me again and told me, "One of the boys called me '*kushi.*'"

"And how did you feel?"

This time his answer was different from the one before: "I have a pure soul, and that's what's most important," he said with confidence, and with a smile on his face, he went off to play.

I thanked the *Ribono Shel Olam* for His help. The song of my pure soul began to play inside of me: "Elokai, *the soul that You put in me is pure; You created it, You formed it, You breathed it into me, and You guard it while it is within me, and one day, You will take it from me and restore it to me in the Time to Come. As long as the soul is within me, I will thank You, Hashem, my G-d and G-d of my ancestors, Master of all works, Lord of all souls. Blessed are You, Hashem, who restores souls to lifeless bodies.*"

And then I said in my own words:
"My thanks to You, Ribono Shel Olam,
That I finally found what's been missing so long.
My thanks to You, Who sits on High,
For all the days You were by my side.
My thanks to You, My Father Above,
Caring and faithful like a pure white dove.
My thanks to You, the Source of my might,
Who took me from darkness and brought me to light."

I had finally emerged from the fog into the light, but even then, I couldn't forget my own people who had not yet discovered the light of their pure souls as I had and were still far away and alienated. Not all of them were able to handle the blow to their identity. Many of us continued to search, and many came to identify with the blacks from other countries and followed in their path. I am not condemning anyone, but I hurt for my dear brothers who lacked the tools to resist and adopted other identities in place of their own. My heart bleeds for them, and I pray to Hashem to strengthen them and help them return to the path their ancestors had walked before them for generations.

CHAPTER THIRTY-SEVEN

A New Beginning

Yehudit's question led me to so many insights, and this led me to write the story of my life in the hope that this book would help other Jews. I endured so much pain and suffering, but it was all worth it to finally make peace with myself.

Today, I know that I am the only one responsible for my life. There are people I recall wounding me deeply over the years, but now I see them as messengers placed in my path to help me grow personally and spiritually.

I decided to write my life story so that other Jews would not give up their identities. An identity builds a person and connects him to the community he wants to be part of. A person should be proud of himself and guard the *tzelem Elokim* within, and not try to redo this *tzelem* for any external reason.

A Jew will always remain a Jew, and he will always swim against the current. Sometimes, a person is afraid to be revealed as himself, but if a person is connected to himself, he will find the good within.

About a year after my conversation with Yehudit, I met her in the playground and thanked her once again. "Yehudit, thank you," I told her. "I can't tell you how much you have helped me."

Yehudit stopped me with a wave of her hand and said, "Please stop, you don't need to thank me all the time." I felt compelled to tell Yehudit all that had happened in the wake of her question. Only a year had passed since that day, but it seemed like much longer. "Yehudit, I went through so much starting from your question. You asked me why it hurt me so much, and your question came exactly at the right time. I had to get to the bottom of it, and in your merit, Yehudit, I dug down and searched, and I can't describe to you the changes that came about as a result of that."

I told Yehudit about the pain I had been suppressing for so many years, and that only at the age of thirty-two was I able to bring it out. Late at night, while the rest of my family was sleeping, I wrote out my story while my tears wet the pages.

"Writing my book gave me so much, and after I finish it, I will be in an even better place. The grief will be behind me," I told Akiva.

"Send us your bill," he joked with his typical sense of humor.

Writing this book was very difficult for me, but I knew that it was an important part of the healing process. After I began writing it, I was able to stage a confrontation between myself and my emotions, and I arrived at many new insights. That night, after parting from Yehudit, I turned to *Hakadosh Baruch Hu* and said, "*Ribono Shel Olam*, I am dust and ashes, flesh and blood. I give my words to You in the hope that You will accept them. *Baruch Hashem*, I am finally relieved of the pain in my heart, and now there is room there to feel the suffering of others. You know my pain so well, as You were with me all the time and helped me to overcome it."

As I was *davening*, an image floated up in my mind of a tree I had encountered during our journey to Eretz Yisrael. It was large and full, and I remember enjoying its shade during a day of rest. I also remember that my mother thanked Hashem for giving us the tree. This tree, which gave us physical support during our troubles, was like the spiritual support I relied on when I came to Eretz Yisrael: I leaned on Hashem.

A New Beginning

"Hashem, You are the Tree I leaned on and am still leaning on until today. You are the Tree that gives me sweet fruits, even if they didn't look that way to me in the past. You are the One Who spreads His shade over me. I will bless You with a *tefillah* that relates to my life experiences. This is how my mother blessed our tree, and so I say today: May it be Your will that all Your beloved children that You chose above all others should go in Your ways, and that those of Your children who have not yet tasted the sweetness of Your fruit should merit to taste them, and their sweetness should always remain within them."

There once was a King, unique, a Foundation,
Who went out to choose for Himself His own nation.
"Is it Me you will serve?" He asked them. "It's your choice."
"We will do and then listen," they said with one voice.
This King, so unlike all the others,
Saw them as His children, and they were all brothers.
He fulfilled all their needs with grace and with ease,
And gave them whatever it was that they pleased.
He cared for them all, from eldest to child,
Clothed them and fed them all the while.
In times of war, He vanquished their foes,
While they sat on the sidelines, relieved of their woes.
They were His servants, faithful and true,
And they guarded their King and gave Him His due.
But the days went by, and it came to a point,
When other kings they began to anoint.
Slowly, they started to veer off their path,
And the gifts of their King they rejected with wrath.
They distanced themselves from their Merciful King,
But found no replacement, no golden ring.

We, Am Yisrael, are His servants, Baruch Hu,
We turned from our King and lost ourselves, too.
And now we are mired in a bitter exile,
We turn to our King, and ask without guile:
"Perhaps we have strayed, over the years,
In the fields of strangers, despite all our fears.
To our great sorrow, we rejected Your gifts,
And turned from Your mitzvot with conceit and with rifts.
"Now we are begging You to let us return,
Give us Your hand, so we shouldn't get burned.
Please accept our heartfelt prayer,
That Your House should be built for ever and ever.
Return us, Hashem, place us under Your wing,
For it is You we long for, our One and Only King."

I continued my prayer: "Please, *Ribono Shel Olam*, arise from Your resting place. Prove to the world that You exist, that You are Hashem, that You are the King of the entire world. Look upon our holy forefathers that faithfully followed You, and see the great people among us in whose merit we will all be redeemed. Reveal Your Face, unite us and establish Your House.

"My solace was brought to me through my friend Yehudit, and I extend my hand to You, Hashem, Mitzllal's small hand, and Rachel's adult hand. The two of us are extending our hands, wishing for You to receive the consolation that we found."

CHAPTER THIRTY-EIGHT

Will My Dream Come True?

One evening, I had a dream. In my dream, I saw a small girl, about seven years old, playing with her friends. Suddenly, the girl noticed a black spot in the sky. The spot got smaller and smaller until there was nothing left, and the sky returned to clear blue. The girl continued to look up at the sky and shouted at her friends, "Look! They're leaving Egypt! Can you see it?" Then, a light appeared in the exact same place, and it grew stronger, and with it appeared a shining book. The book opened, and in clear letters were the verses of Chapter Two in *Chumash Shemot*. The light grew brighter and brighter. The girl shut her eyes against the brilliant light, but it seeped through her eyelids and blinded her.

Suddenly, she heard a Voice. The girl couldn't understand what was being said, but she was certain about Who was speaking.

The girl murmured, "I'm sorry! I'm sorry if I sinned in Your eyes!" and struck her heart. The Voice continued speaking, and the girl quieted. "It's not respectful to interrupt," she said to herself. The girl didn't understand what was being said until she heard four words clearly: "I am going now."

The girl opened her eyes slowly and saw that she was no longer a girl, but a mother, and she saw two figures approaching: a small boy of seven dressed in a *glima* (a white caftan worn by rabbis) and holding a staff in his right hand, and on his left was a tall man. As they came closer, the dream faded and I woke up.

I had this dream the night of 22 Sivan, 5769 (June 14, 2009). After several weeks went by and I was still troubled by the dream, I decided to speak with my mother, who knew how to interpret dreams. I told my mother about my dream and described my dismay over the words I had heard. "Why has Hashem abandoned me now?" I asked. "I feel that He is not with me. I have felt Hashem's Presence clearly inside of me my entire life. Now, I feel as if Hashem has left the place within me where He had dwelled all this time, so to speak."

My mother, with her special wisdom, replied with confidence, "Rachel, the black spot you saw in the sky represents the pain and suffering you felt because of the *safek*. The spot disappeared, and light came in its place. You don't suffer the way you did in the past. Hashem told you that He is going, but He isn't; He is still with you, deep in your heart. He is the One Who brought you from the darkness into the light. Hashem said, 'I am going,' because He saw that you were afraid to hear His voice, like the Jews at *Mattan Torah* feared His voice.

"He wants to calm you down, but the truth is that He is still with You. Hashem wants You to make a place for Him, not just in times of suffering, but also in times of joy. Hashem came to tell you that the day is coming when you will see your dream come true, and the small boy you saw dressed in a *glima* and with a staff in his hand will be the leader of the Jewish people, and everyone will listen to him."

My mother's words comforted me, and I *davened* with all my heart, "Abba, please don't test me!" I'd already passed one test, but I was afraid that I wouldn't pass the next one. I recalled my dream, prayed, and wished to see the redeemer of Israel rise and enter his Temple with my own eyes. When that day comes, we will all join in song and dance, musicians will enter the House of the King, His Eternal Home, and all of Am Yisrael will follow, like one man with one heart!

I found my real identity card: *I am a Jew!* Through the *safek* that was imposed upon me, I came to know myself and how unique I am. I was reconnected with my roots.

I pray for my Jewish brothers, who don't know or forgot that they are Jews, to find their way back just as I have. I am so happy to be a part of the Jewish people and a wonderful family, and it should be so for every Jewish man and woman!

CHAPTER THIRTY-NINE

Coming Full Circle

I remember the day we left our home in Ethiopia as if it were yesterday. Twenty-eight years have passed since that spring day. Many of the Beta Yisrael live in Eretz Yisrael, and every year for the *Shalosh Regalim*, crowds ascend to their beloved Yerushalayim where they pray and pour out their hearts at the Kotel Hama'aravi.

Today, as opposed to the past, I hear of many young Ethiopians who are growing in their Judaism. Many are learning in yeshivot and high schools and are learning more about their Jewish identity. I know how difficult taking this step can be, and I'd like to take this opportunity to say that I am proud of you, my brothers and sisters. I admire the strength you've gathered to return to your roots.

All nine families that lived in Adi Teleke now live in Eretz Yisrael; seven live in Kiryat Gat and two in Arad. My parents are fortunate to have had Kayas Goyaitai *z"l*, who hid the knife inside the *sefer Torah*, as a neighbor, along with his family.

Abba and Daniel were reunited in Eretz Yisrael, and today they live in the same city and see each other every day in the local *beit haknesset*. Ima, Aunt Yejevnesh, and Aunt Avishai were also lucky enough to be able to keep in touch, and they regularly attend each other's *simchot*.

The baby born to Aunt Avishai at the beginning of our journey is married and is building a *bayit ne'eman b'Yisrael*. Mosfun, the little boy who was frightened by the shots fired by Setay and his friends, is also married and lives in Be'er Sheva with his family.

Savta Indaya *z"l* did not live to see Eretz Yisrael and Yerushalayim, but she is buried here. Once a year, her children, grandchildren, and great-grandchildren convene at her gravesite, *davening* and recalling stories of her good deeds and her sterling character.

Uncle Kakhsai *z"l*, who was in prison, never came to Eretz Yisrael, and we don't know where he is buried. His family, however, did make it to Eretz Yisrael, and his children and grandchildren live here.

Nogosa, my brother who tended the sheep as a child, is married and lives with his family in Kiryat Gat. He once returned to visit Ethiopia, and there he visited the home of Savta Indaya and Uncle Kakhsai. When he was there, he encountered Savta's Muslim neighbors who flooded him with stories about Savta.

I, Rachel, live with my family in a wonderful neighborhood in Beit Shemesh, surrounded by a very special community.

I saw the value of publicizing my story because I wanted to show the Israeli public a picture of the Ethiopian Jews who live among them. The matter of the *safek* still stings, in one way or another, every one of them, from the oldest to the youngest.

Besides for the *safek*, Ethiopians are faced with other difficult challenges, as well. I wanted to be their spokesperson and spread the message that we need to be sensitive to others—even when they are different from us. Everyone has his or her own struggles, and we have to try not to add to them.

In the past, I had sought to build barriers between myself and other Jews. From my personal experiences, I learned to live with them without barriers because we are all brothers, heart and soul.

I will end with a short *tefillah* to Hashem: May it be Your will that Am Yisrael should merit to fulfill the words: "*How good and pleasant it is for brothers to dwell together…*"

Our house in Ethiopia

Our oven in Ethiopia

Grave of Savta Indaya in Ethiopia

Savta Indaya

My Uncle Kakhsai, who was taken by the Ethiopian government and never returned

Our Muslim neighbors in Ethiopia

My mother with her older brother, David Kakhsai, holding her nephew Issachar